After the Flight 93 Election

MICHAEL ANTON

AFTER THE FLIGHT 93 ELECTION

The Vote that Saved America and What We Still Have to Lose

New York · London

CONTENTS

PREFACE

This volume contains two previously published essays, preceded by one new one. The central piece – "The Flight 93 Election" – is, so to speak, the reason we're here. It was written in two days in August 2016 and published online by the *Claremont Review of Books* on September 5, 2016 – Labor Day.

At first it received little notice, in line with my expectations. It was (somewhat infamously) published pseudonymously. I assumed – and still believe – that half the reason anyone reads anything is because of who wrote it. Conceal an author's identity, lose half your potential readers. Second, those few who recognized my pseudonym ("Publius Decius Mus") would have been readers of a by-then defunct blog, the *Journal of American Greatness,* to which I contributed under the *nom de net* "Decius." Such readers, I further assumed, would consider (as I did) the new piece to be little more than a rehash of my old *JAG* posts.

Two days went by without a peep. Then on September 7, Rush Limbaugh read "The Flight 93 Election" in its entirety on the air. The *CRB*'s website instantly crashed – as did that of *American Greatness* (a successor of sorts to *JAG*), which published the piece concurrently with the *CRB*.

My intent in writing "The Flight 93 Election" was to impress upon those who consider themselves principled conservatives the urgency of the moment and the stakes of the 2016 election, not just for conservatism but for the country. I cannot say to what extent I succeeded, except to note that numerous people have contacted me in the intervening two years to tell me that the piece changed their vote or steeled their resolve. Many others have told me that it "woke them up" to the dangers that militant leftism poses to our country and our civilization. To all those who have thanked me for writing it and wished me well, I here return your thanks.

Of course, "The Flight 93 Election" was (and still is) attacked far more than praised. The substance of those attacks crystalized immediately as the piece gained fame, and I responded to them in a follow-up, entitled "Restatement on Flight 93," published on the *CRB* website on September 13, 2016 (and here republished as the final part of this volume). While the criticism keeps coming, very little is beyond the scope of that initial response. Most of it echoes charges already made during the hectic first few days of the original essay's viral notoriety.

Most, but not all. Over time, a deeper criticism (friendly and otherwise) has emerged. "The Flight 93 Election" is accused of being bereft of any positive vision – a vivid jeremiad, perhaps, but all nightmare, no dream.

In fact, "The Flight 93 Election" was inspired and

informed by exactly such a positive vision – or, more precisely, by an account of America, how and why it is good, whence that goodness derives, and why it deserves to be conserved. I feared that this account – and *a fortiori* the underlying principles and institutions of which it gives account – were at grave risk from the relentless malevolence of their enemies and the fecklessness and errors of their supposed defenders. That fear has abated but little.

Defending America and the West is thought to be the province of "conservatism." Yet the behavior of conservatism's leading spokesmen in 2016 and beyond has cast significant doubt on whether it or they are capable of fulfilling that mission. Certainly, one must wonder what understanding of conservatism would make its adherents so willing to hand our country over to conservatism's, and to America's (at least as we have known her), avowed enemies.

In my view, the urgent task in September 2016 was to demonstrate the folly of that position and shine a spotlight on what we needed to *prevent*. Going forward, we will also need a clearer statement of what we are *for* – and a better awareness of the specific ways it is threatened.

In this spirit of positivity, I here offer a "Pre-Statement on Flight 93." This new essay is placed first for what Aristotle might call its "ontological priority." Though written last (in August 2018, substantially revised in October), it comes first in the logical order of the argument.

Its first two-thirds say nothing I have not believed for at least two decades. But the last third reflects a growing alarm at the Left's intensifying radicalization. I wrote the first draft after President Trump nominated Brett Kavanaugh to the Supreme Court but before the Democrats and the Left launched their disgraceful calumnies against him, aiming not merely to sink his nomination but to destroy his good name. I always expect the Left to behave badly – very badly – but their treatment of this fine man shocked even me.

"The Flight 93 Election" was and continues to be widely ridiculed for its alleged apocalypticism. The following passage struck many as particularly overwrought:

> A Hillary presidency will be pedal-to-the-metal on the entire progressive-Left agenda, plus items few of us have yet imagined in our darkest moments. Nor is even that the worst. It will be coupled with a level of vindictive persecution against resistance and dissent hitherto seen in the supposedly liberal West only in the most "advanced" Scandinavian countries and the most leftist corners of Germany and England. We see this already in the censorship practiced by the Davoisie's social media enablers; in the shameless propaganda tidal wave of the mainstream media; and in the personal destruction campaigns – operated through the former and aided by the latter – of the social justice warriors. We see it in Obama's flagrant use of the IRS to torment political opponents, the gaslighting denial by the media, and the collective shrug by everyone else.
>
> It's absurd to assume that any of this would stop or slow – would do anything other than massively intensify – in a Hillary administration. It's even more ridiculous to expect that hitherto useless conservative opposition would suddenly become effective. For two generations at least, the Left has been calling everyone to their right Nazis. This trend has accelerated exponentially in the last few years,

helped along by some on the right who really do seem to merit – and even relish – the label. There is nothing the modern conservative fears more than being called "racist," so alt-right pocket Nazis are manna from heaven for the Left. But also wholly unnecessary: sauce for the goose. The Left was calling us Nazis long before any pro-Trumpers tweeted Holocaust denial memes. And how does one deal with a Nazi – that is, with an enemy one is convinced intends your destruction? You don't compromise with him or leave him alone. You crush him.

Given what the Left has done – and pledges to continue to do – to Justice Kavanaugh, and indeed to anyone who stands in the way of their lust for unchecked power, can anyone seriously argue that this assessment was wrong? To answer a different question that I'm still occasionally asked: no, I don't regret a word.

These are dangerous times. The Left has made them so and insists on increasing the danger. Leftists hold virtually every commanding height in our society – financial, intellectual, educational, cultural, administrative – and yet they affect the posture of an oppressed and besieged "resistance."

Nonsense. The *real* resistance is led by President Trump. It is resistance to the Left's all-consuming drive for absolute power, its hostility to all American and Western norms – constitutional, moral, prudential – and its boundless destructive enmity. If I have been persuaded by any criticism of "The Flight 93 Election," it is that I was ungenerous to Trump. The president stands clearly and firmly *against* these virulent attacks on America and firmly *for* the protection of life and liberty, and the promotion of the good life for the

American people. Those are the core responsibilities of any American president. May President Trump continue to fulfill them until the end of his constitutionally won second term.

What the Kavanaugh affair has made clearer to me than ever is that the Left will not stop until all opposition is totally destroyed. The harm they do to people, institutions, mores and traditions is, in their view, not regrettable though unavoidable collateral damage; it is rather an essential element of the project. It's a bit rich to be accused by nihilists of lacking a positive vision. But such is life in 2018. To stand up for truth, morality, the good, the West, America, constitutionalism and decency is to summon the furies.

America cannot long go on like this. Something's gotta give, and something will. What that "something" will be depends in no small part on the actions of men and women of good character, good judgment, and goodwill. Among the most heartening things I've seen in my lifetime was the way the president, the Republican establishment, and most of the conservative movement stood together in the face of what a few took to calling "the Flight 93 Confirmation." In that instance, justice was done. Many more tests are coming. Victory will require not just spirit and spine but the right arguments that explicate the right principles.

For all that lies ahead, let us fortify ourselves with a keener awareness of what we still have left to lose. Which is exactly what inspired me to write "The Flight 93 Election" in the first place.

A Note on "Decius"

"The Flight 93 Election" was, as noted, written under the pseudonym "Publius Decius Mus," the full name of the Roman general after whom I signed – as "Decius" – seventy-one blog posts at the late, lamented *Journal of American Greatness*. Both pseudonymity itself and the choice of Decius have been much ridiculed. In particular, it has been widely snickered that, after all, the real Decius died in battle! How is writing an essay – under cover of pseudonymity, no less – even remotely comparable?

Professor Catherine Zuckert of Notre Dame offers perhaps the most detailed objection to my choice. In a footnote to her essay "Trump as Machiavellian Prince? Reflections on Corruption and American Constitutionalism," Zuckert asserts that "Machiavelli would, no doubt, have been puzzled by Anton's choice of a pseudonym."[1] She then attempts to explain why by looking at three of the four passages in Machiavelli's *Discourses on Livy* in which he discusses "Decius." Contra Zuckert, I contend that Machiavelli would have understood my choice perfectly; indeed, he inspired it.

The name "Decius" actually points to three men in Roman history – grandfather, father, and son – at least two of whom sacrificed themselves in battle for their country. (It is known that the youngest fought at the Battle of Asculum, whence is derived the term "Pyrrhic victory," but sources differ on

---

1 Published in *Trump and Political Philosophy: Patriotism, Cosmopolitanism, and Civic Virtue*, ed. Marc Benjamin Sable and Angel Jaramillo Torres (Palgrave Macmillan, 2018), p. 86*n*11.

whether he died or survived.) Machiavelli discusses the Decii in four chapters of the *Discourses*: II 16, III 1, III 39, and III 45.

The foundational and most famous incident in Decii family history occurred during the Battle of Vesuvius (340 B.C.) – which Machiavelli calls "the most important battle ever waged by the Roman people in any war with any nation" (*Discourses* II 16). According to Livy, on the eve of that battle, the eldest Decius and his co-consul, Manlius Torquatus, both were

> *said to have been visited by the same apparition, a man of greater than human stature and more majestic, who declared that the commander of one side, and the army of the other, must be offered up to the Manes and to Mother Earth; and that in whichever host the general should devote to death the enemy's legions, and himself with them, that nation and that side would have the victory. When the consuls had compared these visions of the night, they resolved that victims should be slain to turn away the wrath of Heaven; and, at the same time, that if the warning of the entrails should coincide with what they had seen in their dream, one or other of the consuls should fulfil the decrees of fate.* [VIII 6.9–11]

When the soothsayers took the auspices, they confirmed the judgment of the apparition, adding the important detail that the sacrifices had been unfavorable only for Decius; auguries for Manlius were spotless. Sure enough, as the battle progressed, the wing of the army under Decius's command began to falter, prompting him formally to "devote" himself to the gods for the good of Rome and the army. The ritual complete, he plunged into the thick of the battle and rallied his troops, whereupon he was killed. But the Romans won.

Forty-five years later, the consul's son of the same name made an almost identical self-sacrifice to ensure Roman victory at the Battle of Sentinum (Livy X 28–29). In *Discourses* III 45, Machiavelli contrasts this action with the strategy of the younger Decius's co-consul, Fabius Maximus Rullianus. Fabius, "judging the slow assault to be more useful, reserv[ed] his thrust to the end" and survived. Machiavelli further observes that the reason Fabius acted when he did was to "acquire ... honor" while still "living." He concludes that "Fabius's mode of proceeding is more secure and more to be imitated."

Zuckert takes this as Machiavelli's summary judgment on the issue of Decian self-sacrifice versus Fabian caution and delay. She even goes so far as to assert that Machiavelli draws the same conclusion in *Discourses* II 16: "Machiavelli compares the intentional sacrifice of his life in battle to inspire courage in his troops first by Publius Decius Mus the elder and then by his son Publius Decius Mus unfavorably to the alternative policy adopted by their fellow consuls Manlius Torquatus and Fabius Rullianus, who held part of their troops in reserve to attack and prevail over a tired enemy."

In fact, Machiavelli says nothing about Torquatus adopting a strategy of patience – not in *Discourses* II 16 or anywhere else. In II 16 he instead equates Decius's self-sacrifice with Torquatus's execution of his own son for insubordination. The opposing armies before Vesuvius, he says, were so equal in "forces" and "virtue" that "it was necessary ... that something extraordinary should arise that would make the spirits of one firm and more obstinate than the other." That "something," he goes on to say, was precisely the self-sacrifice of Decius (and the filicide of Torquatus). In other words, Decian self-sacrifice (and Manlian severity) was *necessary* for the Romans to win the most important battle they ever fought. Machiavelli's silence on Torquatus's patience is all the more striking given that Livy specifically mentions that the consul held back his third line (*triarii*) until the enemy "had tired themselves out and broken or blunted their spears" (VIII 10.1–4). If Machiavelli's overarching intention were to demonstrate and praise patience over self-sacrifice, Livy has here handed him on a silver platter the ideal opportunity to do so. But Machiavelli ignores this gift, instead shifting to an abstract discussion of the three lines of a typical Roman army, and never returns to this story again.

Revisiting *Discourses* III 45, we see that Machiavelli condemns not Decius's self-sacrifice but his impetuosity (an unusual stance for a writer known for his frequent praise of "the impetuous, the quick, the partisan, the spectacular and the bloody," as Leo Strauss puts it).[2] Machiavelli does not even hint that Decius's self-sacrifice was bad for Rome; he says only that it was bad for Decius himself. Similarly, he does not say that Fabius's strategy was better for Rome, only that it was better for Fabius himself.

Zuckert similarly interprets Machiavelli's mention of the Decii in *Discourses* III 1 as an unfavorable judgment on their self-sacrifice. The lesson Machiavelli wishes to impart, she claims, is that "laws and orders are a more reliable way of preventing a people from becoming corrupt than inspiring examples of personal behavior." But what Zuckert poses as a dichotomy Machiavelli presents as complementary. He praises the Decii as men who gave "rare and virtuous examples" that

---

2 *Thoughts on Machiavelli* (The Free Press, 1958), p. 82.

led the Roman republic back to its beginnings so as to ensure it a long life. He says that a republic may be led back to its beginnings "either through the virtue of a man or through the virtue of an order" and goes on to say that "such orders have need of being brought to life by the virtue of a citizen who rushes spiritedly to execute them against the power of those who transgress them." In other words, orders and men are both necessary and neither is superior to the other: virtuous men are necessary to execute good orders. Machiavelli drives the point home at the end of the chapter, where he announces that the theme of Book III will be to "demonstrate to anyone how much the actions of particular men made Rome great and caused many good effects in that city."

Zuckert does not mention Machiavelli's most extensive and notable discussion of "Decius," which occurs in *Discourses* III 39.[3] There Machiavelli recounts that the first Decius, before he was consul, served as military tribune to A. Cornelius Cossus, who imprudently led his army into a defile where it was in danger of being surrounded. Recognizing the danger, Decius also saw that the enemy had left unoccupied a nearby hill from which it would be possible to threaten the enemy army in such a way that it could not prevent the Romans' escape. Machiavelli attributes Decius's perspicacity to his possession of "firm science"[4] – that is, to his knowledge of

---

3 Machiavelli indicates the importance of this chapter by contriving to make it one of only two in the entire work in which his two most important symbolic numbers co-occur: in addition to being the 39th chapter of Book III, it is also the 132nd of the *Discourses* overall.

4 This word "science" appears twice in this chapter, nowhere else in the *Discourses* and nowhere in *The Prince*, but twice in *Art of War* in similar contexts.

the general and of particulars, and of how to deduce the former from observation and experience of the latter. This same Decius who later saves a Roman army through self-sacrifice first saves a Roman army by means of "firm science." Machiavelli thus indicates that there are things to learn from, and worthy of imitation in, the examples of both Fabius *and* Decius.

In his monumental *Thoughts on Machiavelli*, Leo Strauss argues that Machiavelli adopts "Fabius" as his "model."[5] In challenging the orthodoxy of his time, Machiavelli imitates "Fabius" by adopting a strategy of caution and delay: "choosing the safer way, [Fabius] gained a more gladdening victory, remaining alive, than the victory which Decius gained by his death. For Decius, imitating his father, sacrificed himself for the expiation of the Romans."[6] Machiavelli imitates Fabius most obviously by waiting to publish his revolutionary books until after his death, sparing himself the persecution that would otherwise have ensued. Like Fabius, he secures his physical safety while still serving his country. He imitates Fabian patience also by implementing an "enterprise" (*Discourses* I, proem) that he knows will take decades and perhaps centuries to bear fruit.

But as Harvey Mansfield has noted, beyond the many things in Machiavelli's work that Strauss "found" and pointed out, there are many others that he "left to be found."[7] In the sentence immediately preceding the one quoted above, Strauss says that "Machiavelli combines the imitation of Jesus with the imitation of Fabius." In other words, Machia-

---

5 *Thoughts on Machiavelli*, pp. 106–7, 152–54, and 165. Cf. pp. 118, 132, 157, and 316n47. The word "model" appears in Strauss's text thirty-nine times.
6 Ibid., p. 173.

7 *Machiavelli's Virtue* (University of Chicago Press, 1996), p. 228.

velli utilizes more than one model. Might he imitate still other models? A moment's reflection suffices to recognize the core similarity between Jesus and Decius. Are there other similarities?

Machiavelli imitates Jesus in being an "unarmed prophet" (*Prince* 6) – that is, unlike Moses, he lacks physical arms, but like Jesus he wields spiritual arms. But a key theme of both the *Discourses* and *The Prince* (especially of *Prince* 14) is the equivalence of knowledge and arms, which one may say for Machiavelli replaces the classical equivalence of knowledge and virtue. Decius's "firm science" is then an example of "good arms" (*Prince* 12) – of the type of knowledge that can win "in the temporal" (*Prince* 11).

Machiavelli – even more than his Decian character – possesses "firm science," which he intends to use to save his people. Indeed, he judges that *only* "firm science" can save his people. But it can do so only if they can be made to listen. Machiavelli's enterprise requires new modes and orders, which requires the abolition of existing modes and orders. Previous attempts to break the suffocating hold of existing authority (for instance, by Dante and Marsilius of Padua, and by the humanists) were too timid, too cautious, too weak. Strauss says that Machiavelli's true addressees are the youth with the potential to break the impasse. But they

> have been brought up in teachings which, in the light of
> Machiavelli's wholly new teaching, reveal themselves to be
> much too confident in human goodness ... and hence
> much too gentle or effeminate. Just as a man who is tim-
> orous by training or nature cannot acquire courage,
> which is the mean between cowardice and foolhardiness,

> *unless he drags himself in the direction of foolhardiness,*
> *so Machiavelli's pupils must go through a process of bru-*
> *talization in order to be freed from effeminacy.*[8]

Stronger medicine – more potent than any hitherto administered – is required. But such medicine will necessarily shock
and anger. Even – especially – if the medicine is effective at
killing malignant cells, adherents of the existing modes and
orders will damn the doctor's name in perpetuity. He will for
all time be called a devil, an antichrist, a teacher of evil. Like
Decius, Machiavelli sacrifices part of himself – in his view,
the only everlasting part: his reputation, his *nome* – to save
his *patria*. Like Decius (and Jesus), Machiavelli's new orders
can be implemented only through, and after, his death.

One may grant this interpretation (though I am confident
many will not) and still fairly ask what any of it has to do with
me. In 2016, I judged the modes and orders of my time –
and especially of conservatism – to be exhausted and impris-
oned within an inflexible institutional and intellectual
authority. I believed that its conclusions on the most press-
ing matters were false and pernicious and that its orthodoxy
therefore required smashing. I believed that ordinary rhetoric would not suffice. I knew that in writing I would anger
many more than I inspired. In Machiavelli's words:

> *nothing is more difficult to handle, more doubtful of suc-*
> *cess, nor more dangerous to manage, than to put oneself*
> *at the head of introducing new orders. For the introducer*
> *has all those who benefit from the old orders as enemies,*

---

8 *Thoughts on Machiavelli*, pp. 81–82.

and he has lukewarm defenders in all those who might benefit from the new orders.... Consequently, whenever those who are enemies have opportunity to attack, they do so with partisan zeal, and the others defend lukewarmly so that one is in peril along with them. [*Prince* 6]

I had no expectation that pseudonymity would hold; it was merely an expedient, a short-term Fabianism useful in the moment but certain to end. I therefore knew or believed that I would forever close many doors. I would lose friends, old and new. A very large part of the "conservatism" I was trying to rouse would come to hate me. I would be – sooner rather than later – ending a reasonably successful corporate career, with no possibility of its ever being revived. My future employment prospects would become at best uncertain. I would be called terrible things ("authoritarian," "anti-Semitic," "white nationalist," "racist"). My name would become synonymous with a politics that half the country and all our elites denounce as evil. All of this – and more – did in fact occur.

Yet unlike for Machiavelli, the issue could not wait. The moment required a decision, which required public deliberation, which required a public statement. I had something to say that was not being said, or not sufficiently, that I thought had to be said. I still believe – as I privately concluded then – that it would have been better had someone of greater virtue or reputation said it, and said it better. But in the moment, it did not appear that anyone would.

PRE-STATEMENT ON FLIGHT 93

What follows is not a philosophical treatise; it is a political argument. My aim is to outline the essences of conservatism, Americanism, and Western civilization, and to review the main threats to their survival. I make no claim to philosophic or scholarly definitiveness, much less originality. My goal is to proffer a rallying point for the American Right by summarizing the main ideas and institutions that it should devote itself to preserving and defending. Of necessity, I resort to a not inconsiderable amount of summary, elision, corner-cutting, question-begging, problem-dodging, and oversimplification. Politics goes on whether or not we resolve every – or any – complex philosophical debate. Some of those debates, indeed, are unresolvable.

But human beings are always forced to act in the here and now. Acting well requires a basis for evaluating options. In the political realm, that basis for evaluation is more properly termed a theory of justice. The Left, as I will try to demonstrate, has such a theory. The Right, as I tried to explain in both "The Flight 93 Election" and the "Restatement on Flight 93," thinks it does but does not.

But we need one. We cannot win either the intellectual argument or the political struggle without one. While the need for something is no guarantee of its availability, I am optimistic that this particular need can be met. There is under our very noses a theory of justice that is both logically coherent and distinctively American. This theory helped to build and sustain the greatness of our nation over centuries. Upon it we can rebuild a conservatism that is actually conservative, that seeks to – and that can – conserve America, its people, its communities, its ideas, its traditions, and what is best and truest in Western civilization.

The ideas I here lay out may seem familiar and obvious to many readers. But they require restatement because, in my estimation, the errors and failures of conservativism nearly all arise from forgetting, insufficiently understanding, never knowing, or denying the claims to truth that I shall assert.

Political and Moral Epistemology

Aristotle begins both his *Politics* and his *Nicomachean Ethics* with the sensible and true observation that all human activity aims at some good. Our activity therefore presupposes that the good exists and that it is knowable. Most men, most of the time, simply assume they know what is good. Mostly this comes down to knowing what they want and assuming it is good, or assuming that their own particular ways and habits are good.

Political philosophy was born when some men, instead of simply identifying the good with the objects of human desire or with their own customs and traditions, began an inquiry to discover the true human good. That inquiry presumes that human nature and the human good can be discovered and known – or at least better known, if perhaps never fully and finally known – through reasoned analysis.

It is important to understand that any account of good and bad, right and wrong, justice and injustice that does not begin from these premises is *ipso facto* nonrational. Reject this starting point and one is left with only two alternatives: either take guidance from a revealed account of the good and what it commands, or assert that justice is simply a matter of human will – i.e., assert that justice does not exist independent of preference and choice but is simply whatever this or that people in this or that time says it is. Tradition offers no reassurance because tradition without a rational basis is, in the last analysis, just an unconscious resort to will.

But "nonrational" does not necessarily mean "irrational." A rational account of justice is not inherently incommensurable with a revealed account. It is true that philosophy at the highest level refuses to submit to any authority and insists on independently investigating every claim to truth. Revelation, by contrast, holds that the true account of the human good begins from God's Word, which reason is incapable of fully understanding and which it is impious to question. Yet it would be strange if the Creator's commandments did not accord with rationally discoverable moral principles. It would be equally strange if the reasoned investigation of morality in a created world could discern no rational moral principle at all. Modern natural science has shown that the physical world is governed by discoverable laws that accurately predict the behavior of much in and of that world. Why cannot something similar be true for the human world, and more specifically the moral world?

One might object by noting that moral philosophy – which lacks the methodology, controlled experiments, and mathematical tools of natural science – is inherently inexact and surmise from this that its conclusions are questionable at best, invented at worst. But this difference in precision does not require that moral philosophy be dismissed as untrue, as merely a matter of opinion, relative to time and place or particular to a certain people. To justify such a dismissal, one would first have to establish that natural science and moral philosophy share an essential epistemological commonality requiring that they be investigated in the same way. One must further prove that the methodology of natural science is the only valid way to investigate moral and political things. To say the least, this has not been demonstrated. To the contrary, two millennia of deep inquiry have shown that an account of justice need not rest on the modern scientific method in order to be fully rational. Aristotle, indeed, admonishes that for all inquiries we should "seek out precision in each genus to the extent that the nature of the matter allows" and makes clear that the proper way to investigate ethics and politics is dialectically, and not what we today would term "scientifically."

By contrast, any account of justice based on human will is inherently irrational. One might be tempted to say that the very decision to will into being "justice" in the face of moral nihilism is itself rational, because *something* is better than *nothing*. But this assertion is problematic for two reasons. First, that decision would be rational only if it were *known* that justice does not exist apart from will. But this has not been proved. Second, even – or especially – in the face of such certainty, one must wonder why it would be good to will "justice" into being. If moral nothingness were known to be true, then any moral "something" that is merely a creation of human will would be not merely false but *known* to be false. Indeed, by what standard could one even assert a true difference between better and worse? The choice for a willed "justice" over nihilism, for something over nothing, would therefore itself be merely an act of will.

Much more plausible – and therefore rational, if not "scientifically" provable – is an account of the human good that begins from what we can observe about man and draws provisional conclusions, investing increasing confidence in those conclusions as they are continually subjected to dialectical and empirical critique and revision.

Human Nature, Mere Life, and the Good Life

A cursory glance at humanity finds a multiplicity of different peoples living according to a wide variety of distinct laws, customs, traditions, religions, and so on. From this diversity some suppose that – apart from the biological similarity of human bodies – there is nothing essentially human at all, certainly nothing that might enable one to deduce standards of good and bad or right and wrong from human nature.

In fact, however, scant reflection suffices to discern commonalities across all human populations. All human beings are driven by a mixture of appetites, passions, and reason, in varying degrees and relative combinations. Some of these – e.g., appetites for food and sex – we share with the other animals. Others – e.g., desire for glory and envy of others' successes – are distinctly human. But the essentially human characteristics, the ones that most separate man from all the other known beings, are the capacity for speech and reasoning, and the sociability that flows therefrom.

This difference is one of kind and not merely degree: man is not just a clever ape. He is something distinct from and above the apes, and indeed all animals. He is a natural being but also the source of all in the world that is not natural: laws, customs, traditions, and the arts (understood both as the means of providing useful things – clothing, tools, etc. – and as expressions of man's creativity, such as poetry and music). Man is furthermore the only known part of nature that is *aware* of nature, that can recognize the distinction between nature and non-nature, that can wonder about the existence of the universe and his own place within the whole. He is the only natural being that can ask the questions "What is good for me?" and "How should I live?"

The first and most obvious answer to these questions is that one must preserve and sustain life itself, since the good life presupposes mere life. If there is a good life, then life itself must be good, for the good life could not exist without mere life. For the same reason, the things that protect and sustain life must also be good. The human good therefore begins with the protection of our bodily life from external dangers: from natural predators and cataclysms, from drought, famine, and flood, and also from the depredations of other humans. Those depredations may occur *absent* political society, in a "war of all against all" in which men lack any effective machinery to govern behavior and to deter and punish injustice; they may happen *within* a political society, the more so when the government is too weak or incompetent to prevent some from doing injury to others; or they may happen *to* a political society in the form of foreign conquest, raids, and the like.

Human life is not sustainable without a modicum of material goods. And for man to live as man, as distinct from beast, these material needs extend beyond food and water to include things such as shelter, clothing, and medicine. These in turn require the development and flourishing of basic arts and sciences.

Such are the conditions for *mere* life, but what are the conditions for the *good* life? Indeed, what *is* the good life? What are its content and contours? How are these to be discovered? Despite the multiplicity of human customs and ways of life, man *qua* man (to repeat) is characterized by certain passions and faculties, above all by reason or speech. Reason enables him to raise the question of the good life and to investigate and evaluate possible answers.

Some of man's passions and appetites not only threaten mere life; they undermine the emergence and flourishing of the good life. The overindulgence of those appetites and passions that tend toward bodily degradation or destruction are to be shunned. Man should not, for example, eat too much, or eat things that are bad for him. For the same reason, neither should he indulge a misguided sense of honor in any act of violence not strictly necessary for his defense or the defense of those close to him or of his community.

Beyond mere life and safety, the good life is defined by happiness or felicity. One source of felicity is the development of the higher faculties through education to realize the potential of our innate capabilities. Education in turn requires not just the "safe harbor" of security but also the cultivation of the higher arts and sciences that can only flourish within, and are characteristic of, civilization.

Education is not simply the study of theoretical science, technical facts, or useful arts, although these are necessary and good. Education is concerned above all with the virtues: particularly moderation, justice, courage, and wisdom. The virtues are, in a sense, reason made manifest – the qualities and behaviors that flower when man is at his best, his most human and most rational. Nor is education simply a matter of formal schooling. Virtue is inculcated at many levels of society – in schools, of course, but also in the family, in religious and civic institutions, in the workplace, and within friendships.

Virtue, law, government, education, the arts and sciences – in short, civilization – must be cultivated, but they are also natural to man in that man cannot be fully or essentially man without them. What is "natural" to man includes those things that make man who he really is: a being that is by nature social, political, and (at least potentially) rational. In other words, civilization is ontologically natural to man, even though he must build and maintain it himself.

Nature itself, or human nature, thus sets the standard for how man should live. That standard is not self-evident in the sense of its every contour being immediately obvious to all. But it is discoverable and teachable by philosophers; it can be popularized and disseminated by poets, playwrights, novelists, and teachers; and it can be approximated by political men in the crafting of laws. Indeed, we may judge the goodness of a law by how closely it conforms to the natural standard, or by how well it conduces to that standard for a given people at a given time.

Human nature has a goal or end: the completion or perfection of those traits which are uniquely characteristic of man. Clearly, "perfection" is a standard more to be striven for than actually achieved. Just as clearly, human beings vary in their capacity to acquire and develop the virtues. Not all are equally able to develop the virtues to the same degree, and some may be incapable of participating in certain virtues at all. It would be absurd, for instance, to expect everyone to be equally courageous, or to be equally capable of achieving wisdom.

Yet all human beings are capable of practicing justice and moderation, and perhaps a modicum of many other virtues as well. The goal for any individual, therefore, is to cultivate those virtues within reach to the greatest extent possible. This, again, requires law, education, the family, civil and religious institutions, arts and sciences, etc. – i.e., civilization. Maintaining and preserving these must therefore be a part of man's duty. As Aristotle says, man is the best of animals when completed, but the worst of all when separated from law and the judicial order.

The American Solution

This view of human nature and the morality arising therefrom was shared, more or less, by philosophers and political men for more than two thousand years. This is not to deny important differences between ancient and modern political theory and practice. It is, however, to caution against making more of those differences than is warranted. Hobbes, for instance, attacks Aristotle frequently and with relish, but also condemns his own (in)famous "state of nature" as the enemy of life, civilization, and "felicity" – a thought not unlike the one cited from Aristotle above.

Philosophic controversies aside, justice in the real world takes form in actual countries, through governments and laws. These should be judged according to how effectively they protect their citizens' lives, liberties, and property, and by how well they enable or facilitate the fulfillment of each individual's natural ends. In other words, by how effectively they protect their people's *safety* and promote their *happiness*.

Let us, in that spirit, examine how – and how well – the American founders and their successors (particularly Lincoln and his heirs) solved the fundamental political problem: building a regime that secures mere life while facilitating and encouraging the good life.

The founders begin from the fact of human equality, which they deduce from the rational investigation of human nature. Man is defined by those traits or qualities that distinguish him from all other beings, lower and higher, and all men are found to be equal in this decisive respect. They are by nature equally free and independent. Equality and liberty are thus inherently joined, two sides of the same coin. Men are equal in being by right (if not always in fact) equally free of domination by others, and they are justly free because they are naturally equal.

Unlike social insects, human beings are not naturally differentiated into rulers and ruled. This is obvious from the fact that – unlike in the case of, say, bees – nature does not clearly distinguish human workers from masters in ways that men acknowledge and accept. No man – even of the meanest capacities – ever consents to slavery, which can be maintained only with recourse to the lash.

Certainly, nature blesses or endows some individual men with greater ability to govern, and/or with superior virtue, which makes them more deserving of the honor. Yet nature produces no perfectly just and wise men – the only kind who might be entitled by nature to rule – which means that no man may justly rule any other without that other's consent. No man may injure any other or infringe on another's rights, except in just defense of his own rights. The existence of equal natural rights entails an equally natural duty that all men respect the identical rights of others. Indeed, the only way to enjoy our rights is to fulfill our duties.

Because men are driven by passions as well as reason, and by vice as well as virtue, the temptation to violate the rights of others is always present, especially in the strong. Men in the state of nature – that is, without government, whether understood as a pre-political state or following the dissolution of a political order – are free but at grave risk of injury and depredation. Such injuries are not merely bad for individual men, they violate a moral standard that nature provides but leaves to us to enforce.

Moreover, men in the state of nature cannot utilize to their full potential those talents that God and nature have given them. Living well requires not only the society of others, but also security. Men consent to government in order to secure their lives and equal natural rights and to thrive within that security. Upon establishing a government, men conditionally cede some of their natural rights and liberties in order to secure the far larger remainder. For instance, men must surrender to government their natural right to inflict just punishment in redress of injury. This ceding is conditional because our rights remain the gift of God and nature, not of government, and consent may justly be withdrawn if the government fails in its duties or abuses its powers. Therefore, there is an inalienable natural right "to alter or to abolish" an oppressive or incompetent government.

The satisfaction of individual needs and wants is, to an extent, necessary for both mere life and the good life but insufficient for the latter. The sole or highest purpose of society is therefore not the satisfaction of primal wants and needs. The rights that a just political order exists to protect extend above and beyond those necessary merely to preserve and sustain the body. There are, for example, natural rights of free speech and freedom of conscience and association – rights which more fully define man as man than the lower rights to physical security and property. Political society is also necessary for and must be concerned with the flourishing of all higher aspects of human nature, which are undermined by radical individualism and private hedonism. Sound politics – a good regime – therefore strikes a balance between the rights of the individual and the demands of the political community, which is the necessary vehicle for human beings to secure their rights and create a "space" or realm in which all the virtues, arts, and sciences can flourish.

The best way to secure equal natural rights – especially in an expansive country with a multiplicity of interests and localized differences – is through representative republicanism, federalism, the separation of powers, and especially limited government. Each of these is important for complementary reasons. Representative republicanism acknowledges and honors the fundamentally political nature of political questions; that is, it recognizes that some decisions properly belong to the public as a whole and not to any part, and certainly not to any part that claims to speak from authority – religious, scientific, or otherwise. Republicanism is meaningful only if popular majorities have the power to decide political questions, while not infringing on the rights of those in the minority. Republicanism is representative, rather than direct, owing first to the impracticalities of participatory democracy in a large country but more fundamentally to the dangers of majority tyranny and whim, which are moderated as the people's views are refined through representative institutions.

Federalism is both a means of facilitating local decision-making over essentially local issues and a way of disaggregating government power so as to make its concentration and abuse less likely. The separation of powers, also, is a crucial bulwark against tyranny as well as a means of allowing qualitatively different functions of government to be carried out by distinct branches specifically designed for those purposes.

Limited government is not synonymous with "small" government, though a properly limited government will in almost all circumstances be smaller than one not so limited. A limited government is rather one whose powers are circumscribed by fixed boundaries and enumerated powers. The size of a properly limited government can vary with circumstances: bigger government is justified and even necessary to winning a war (i.e., to protecting citizens' lives and liberties). The reason for limiting government is not strictly to keep it small but to keep it focused on its core tasks: securing equal natural rights, protecting persons and property, and creating and maintaining conditions for the good life.

Government also has a role to play in promoting republican virtue through education and support for the integrity and health of the family. In practice, this means respecting the role of religion and religious institutions not only in private life – which is required by the natural right to freedom of conscience – but to a certain extent in public life as well. It means that – despite the incommensurability of reason and revelation at the highest level of thought – there is no inherent conflict between the demands of faith and the requirements of reason in the political realm. It is reasonable that the God who revealed the Decalogue, preached the Sermon on the Mount, and created the natural world also endowed that world with natural moral principles that accord with His law. The alternative – moral commands with no basis in nature or that contradict nature – is irrational and implausible.

Nonetheless, in the modern Western world – which is in part defined by the sharp separation between civil law and religious doctrine – religious and other traditional sources of human guidance cannot be authoritative for politics. Doctrinal controversies between or within faiths have no inherent political relevance and investing them with political significance leads to religious persecution. The existence of multiple faiths and sects requires that politics be grounded in a reasoned account of human nature that admits man's inability to know the mind of God and respects each person's equal natural right to follow his own conscience in matters of worship. This means that only those faiths which recognize and honor the distinction between civil and religious law are compatible with republican government. Similarly, cultural traditions are to be tolerated insofar as they do not contradict natural rights, and celebrated and promoted insofar as they help sustain the habits necessary for republican government.

Scope and Limits of the American Solution

The principles outlined above, while universally valid for all men in all times and places, are subject to practical limits and qualifications.

First, men are equal only in possessing equally the same natural rights. Men naturally differ in virtue, intelligence, talent, and other traits. None of these natural inequalities provides a just title to rule others without their consent. But they do result in inequalities of wealth, honors, social standing, power, etc. – especially when and where equal natural rights to utilize unequal talents are properly secured. Since excellence in husbandry, the arts and sciences, commerce, and many other endeavors is a boon to individuals, to society, indeed to all mankind, this inequality of outcomes is welcome. More important, it is unjust to place arbitrary limits on the natural freedom to exercise one's talents. Yet government has a duty to prevent natural inequality from degenerating into de facto oligarchy; the best way to ensure this is through rigorous, impartial enforcement of the laws.

Second, any social compact – and hence any political community – is inherently particular. Its full privileges extend only to those men who have consented to its terms, and whose membership has been consented to by all other citizen-members. The equal natural rights of all men do not demand or imply world government or open borders. To the contrary, a social compact without limits is impossible, a self-contradiction: a compact that applies indiscriminately to all is not a compact. Since mutual consent is an indispensable foundation of political legitimacy, membership in the political community must be invitation-only. Moreover, just as nature endows men equally with inalienable rights, human nature similarly entitles the nations of the world to a "separate and equal station" with respect to other nations. "As I would not be a slave, so I would not be a master," Lincoln said. Applied to international relations, we may similarly affirm that as no nation is by right a colony, none should be an empire.

Third, form must always fit matter. "Matter" in this sense is the actual country, the "facts on the ground": the people, their language, traditions, customs, and religion(s); the topography, resources, and climate; the geographical site and situation, and relations with neighbors and other world powers. "Form" is the regime, or mode of government, and above all the principles informing that mode. There may be – as ancient philosophers from Plato to Aristotle to Cicero assert – one regime that is simply best. But they add that this best form is not always practicable or possible; it is suitable only for the finest matter, and only in those rare instances where and when circumstances permit.

While the American regime takes its bearings from human nature, this in itself does not mean that it can be successfully applied anywhere, to anyone. It is a perhaps sad but nonetheless intractable truth that not all peoples in all times and places are ready or able to assume the responsibilities of liberty or to secure their equal natural rights through republican government. The particular traditions, customs, laws, talents, education, religious practices, and private habits of a people determine the likelihood of successfully applying the American solution, and thus the wisdom of the attempt. Even the American people themselves were not inherently or immediately capable of creating or sustaining a republican regime. It took well over a century of quasi self-rule via colonial legislatures, plus the crucibles of the French and Indian War and the Revolutionary War, to make us ready for it. The great task before the founders of any government is thus to devise a form as consistent as possible with timeless truths about human nature yet also appropriate to the particular characteristics and circumstances of an actual people at a given time.

Finally, republican government requires a measure of commonality in customs, habits, and opinions. Republicanism is not possible when the people becomes so fractured that private or sectional or group interests override agreement on the common good. The incorporation of new citizens into the social compact is possible and even salutary in certain circumstances, but only if the newcomers possess republican spirit and sufficiently adopt the customs, habits, and opinions of the existing majority. Immigrants must desire and be capable of assimilation – and the country accepting them must insist on it. In determining whether to welcome newcomers and in what numbers, a republic's overriding considerations must always be the preservation of republican habits and institutions plus the well-being and desires of the existing citizenry. Another paramount consideration must be the capacity of the existing citizenry and its institutions and economy to absorb and assimilate newcomers. This capacity varies according to times and circumstances and is never unlimited. In sum, a republic that opens its doors to immigrants must choose carefully whom and how many to accept; it must insist on and impel assimilation; and it must be able and willing to recognize its own limits in successfully assimilating newcomers, and protect its citizenry accordingly.

American Attacks on the American Solution

The American solution has delivered amazing success for the American people – and even for some other peoples who, in emulation, have made their governments more like ours. Yet in spite of this success (or because of it) the American solution has been under attack almost since its inception – from Loyalists and the throne-and-altar Right to Rousseauean romantics and Hegelian historicists, from Marxists to fascists, from the postmodern Left to the paleo Right and beyond.

Three peculiarly American lines of attack concern us most, for two reasons: they share essential common arguments, and they have done the most damage not just to American political thought but to the country itself. Brief sketches of the first two will suffice here, but the third – under which we still live and which is the principal internal threat to the republic in our time – must be explained in some detail.

The first attack was the pre–Civil War denial of the principle of equal natural rights in favor of an assertion of group rights that inhere in political minorities rather than individual human beings. The reason for this attack was of course to defend slavery, to assert and insist that it could never justly be ended by political means – not even by constitutional supermajorities. In this view – most fully articulated by Senator John C. Calhoun of South Carolina – a political minority (in this case, the slave states, but in principle any minority) holds an inalienable right to veto majority will, and even to impose policies over the majority's objection.

That this position is inherently at odds with the principles of the American founding was instantly understood by its adherents and opponents alike. Calhoun would go so far as to denounce the founding principle that "all men are created equal" as "the most dangerous of all political error" and a "self-evident lie." On one level, it is clear why he would so insist: human equality is obviously incompatible with slavery. The deeper reason, perhaps less clear, is that government by consent requires majority rule. Majority opinion at that time sought to keep slavery out of U.S. territories and place it, in Lincoln's words, "in the course of ultimate extinction." Calhoun and his followers thus saw clearly that defending their "peculiar institution" required attacking majority rule. And since majority rule flows axiomatically from equal natural rights, if slavery were to survive in America, human equality would have to be replaced with inequality, individual rights with group rights, and majority rule with minority imposition.

This first attack on the American solution arose largely from self-interest. The second – the Progressivism of the late nineteenth and early twentieth centuries – arose from a new account of human nature and how the human good can be known. Progressivism dismisses the philosophical-dialectical account sketched above in favor of one allegedly based on historical and scientific progress. According to this view, there is no fixed human nature; the human situation is always fundamentally changing, typically for the better, as human beings become more knowledgeable and more capable. In recent times, this progress has yielded (among other achievements) modern social science, which Progressivism claims is precise and rigorous, unlike earlier philosophy, which it condemns as fundamentally imprecise and amorphous.

The original Progressives thus mounted a theoretical critique of core American principles and institutions. They condemned the machinery of American government – such as federalism and the separation of powers – as slow and cumbersome obstacles to progress. They rejected limited government as too narrow to effect what they saw as the necessary expansion of government's powers to cope with an increasingly complex world. But above all, they dismissed the founding principles as timebound and out-of-date, perhaps adequate for the simpler circumstances of the eighteenth century but insufficient to meet the challenges of their own time and especially of later times.

Progressivism asserts that progress in human understanding and the accumulation of knowledge so illuminate formerly obscure subjects that questions once deemed matters of legitimate disagreement, and therefore appropriately decided through political deliberation, become instead assertions that can be shown to be either correct or incorrect. Obviously, only the correct understanding of any issue should inform policy; incorrect understandings have no just claim to do so, even if desired (and enacted) by democratic majorities. Furthermore, as knowledge increases in volume and complexity, it becomes understandable to fewer and fewer, and as the universe of questions with known answers expands, the number of people capable of knowing those answers shrinks. Both dynamics work in tandem to reduce the number of issues properly left to political deliberation and increase the number of those that should be decided and administered by trained experts: the scope of politics thus radically constricts. In Engels's famous formula, "[t]he government of persons is replaced by the administration of things." Except that Engels expected "the administration of things" to lead to the withering away of the state, whereas the wiser Progressives knew that "the administration of things" would require a state larger and more powerful than any hitherto imagined.

Our Elites' Understanding of "Justice"

The third attack on the American solution, post-1960s leftism, draws elements from the earlier two: from the antebellum defenders of slavery, the idea of "group rights"; from the Progressives, the concept of rule by experts through a leviathan state; and from both, the rejection of America's founding principles.

To these it adds a new understanding of justice, derived from the union of two more recent strains of thought: Rawlsian liberalism and the New Left. Both of these emerged from the universities at about the same time, but we may say that the former is a product of the faculty and the latter a creation of the students. They emerged separately but later formed a kind of synthesis when the students became the faculty.

Rawlsian liberalism – brainchild of the Harvard professor John Rawls – judges right and wrong on the basis of "justice as fairness," but on a radically redefined notion of fairness. In the earlier American tradition, fairness meant equal, impartial enforcement of just laws, and majority rule that respects and protects minority rights. But, as we have seen, this understanding leads inevitably to unequal outcomes. Rejecting the older tradition's argument that such inequalities are natural and salutary, Rawlsian liberalism considers them artificial and unjust. It thus creates a distinction between mere "formal" equality – equal treatment before the law – and "genuine" equality: equal outcomes. The purpose of public policy – of government itself – is (or must be made to be) to achieve "genuine" equality through the redistribution of goods such as power, wealth, and honors from the "privileged" to the "disadvantaged." Policies are deemed good only to the extent that they help the disadvantaged – especially the most disadvantaged.

Yet "justice as fairness" also holds that inequalities of wealth, power, and honors may justly be allowed so long as such inequalities benefit the disadvantaged. For those who – through their positions within society or the economy – provide physical, monetary, or even rhetorical benefit to the disadvantaged, greater wealth and honors are not merely justified but good. Indeed, simply holding and promoting correct opinions on the advantage-disadvantage question is enough to justify greater wealth and status. This explains, for instance, why the Left does not merely tolerate but celebrates the massive wealth concentrations and tax-favored status of universities and why it adulates tech CEOs and "woke" celebrities.

The second strain of post-1960s leftism emerged from the New Left and today marches under the banner of "social justice." It incorporates every element of Rawlsian liberalism while finding it too limited. (We here pass over the many specific ways in which Rawls and his heirs have attempted to update their theory in order to keep up with the New Left. Suffice it to say that formal Rawlsianism is always a step or two behind and continues to require a good deal of reactive updating to ensure that it remains compatible with up-to-the-minute leftist assertions, which always take priority.)

"Social justice" lodges three complaints against "justice as fairness": first, that it is insufficiently concerned with the *causes* of disadvantage; second, that it is concerned only with *present* disadvantage and has nothing to say about *past* disadvantage; third, that it focuses on *individual* disadvantage to the exclusion of *group* disadvantage.

These complaints are inextricably related. "Social justice" theory insists that the cause of nearly all disadvantage is oppression – not just overt oppression that everyone can plainly see but also the subtle, institutional oppression that pervades all of society; and not just oppression in the present, but also oppression in the past, the long-term effects of which continue to inflict damage. The suffering of one's ancestors – insofar as that suffering is not outweighed by injustice committed by said ancestors – is decisive for one's fortunes and social position today. This is why it is not enough to aim remedial policies only at individuals; they must be extended across entire demographic groups. The past suffering of any member of a disadvantaged group causes present harm to all members of that group.

The past, then, is not really past. Not only does past injustice continue to cause disadvantage in the present; it also – and perhaps more fundamentally – continues to confer benefits on the descendants of oppressor groups. Those benefits – commonly referred to as "privilege" – are cumulative, hereditary, and perpetual. The past thus continues in the present to work both sides of the ledger: to further disadvantage the disadvantaged, and to further advantage the advantaged. Therefore, one cannot redress present injustice without also redressing past injustice. Even if one could, justice itself would still require the redress of past injustice: the crimes of the past must be answered for.

Privilege and oppression are collective and inherent to groups rather than merely present or absent for individuals. The fact that certain members of a broadly disadvantaged group are objectively more advantaged – in wealth, power, honors, or anything else – than an average person in the privileged class does not in any way mitigate their group disadvantage. The disadvantaged are, as a group, permanent victims of the advantaged. Therefore basic justice – merely achieving a level playing field – requires preferential treatment for every member of a disadvantaged group, regardless of current socioeconomic status. "Social justice" thus requires recourse to the concept of group rights, which was not – at least not originally – a feature of Rawlsian liberalism.

Redistributive policies must go on forever, even if the oppressor group becomes genuinely disadvantaged, because – as one liberal commentator put it – group oppression is a debt that "can never be repaid." Still, the impossibility of full repayment in no way obviates the effort, since justice requires that whatever *can* be repaid *must* be repaid. Not coincidentally, the project of exacting repayment is very effective at unifying the various pleaders, politicians, professionals, and interest groups into a block passionately committed to unlimited government.

Incoherent in Theory, Destructive in Practice

The best thing one can say about the antebellum attack on the American idea is that it was defeated in war before it could attain much influence – that is, until one of its core tenets was picked up by modern leftists more than a century later.

The best thing one can say about the original Progressives is that many within the movement sought specific policies and goals that are fully consistent with core American principles, that would almost certainly have won the approval of the founders and their heirs, and that could have been enacted on the basis of the original tenets of American political thought. It suffices to mention strengthening education at all levels, supporting morality and the family, bolstering the work ethic, immigration and civil service reform, trust-busting to enable fair competition, calls to national service, and the creation of the National Park system. The tragedy of Progressivism is that it mistakenly and unnecessarily upended the firmest basis for republicanism in an attempt to further many essentially republican ends.

Many harmful consequences followed Progressivism's triumph. Federalism and the separation of powers were undermined. The scope and size of government grew exponentially. The executive branch conceived the embryo of a massive fourth branch now known as the "administrative state."

But Progressivism's most baleful consequence has been theoretical. Progressivism subjected the entire political and moral epistemology sketched above – the only sound and logically consistent basis for republican government – to sustained attack and ridicule. That attack was so effective that it is now impossible for any educated person to say, on the basis of traditional religious faith or a shared understanding of permanent human nature, that anything human can be good or bad.

Progressivism instead replaces human nature with "history" and "science." "History" in this understanding is a process – which may or may not have a goal or end – of continual improvement in human affairs (with allowances for occasional backsliding around the margins). The thought and practice – especially the morality – of the present is always superior to that of the past, in part because of accumulated knowledge. We know more, therefore we know better. Progressivism takes its name from this alleged insight.

Progressivism further holds that present knowledge is superior to the thought of the past not only in quantity but in quality. Contemporary thought is sounder and more rigorous – in a word, truer – because it rests on empirical science and its methodology, in contrast to the inherent imprecision of philosophy, which as a consequence of that imprecision never rises above the level of opinion. Progressivism insists that it can apply the methodology of the natural sciences to the human things and come to conclusions superior to those of philosophy and equal in precision to those of natural science.

Few today would argue that this goal has been achieved. Yet the project has entirely succeeded in disqualifying as "knowledge" any thought or conclusion that does not ostensibly rest on the scientific method. This belief that "science" is the highest – and perhaps the only – form of knowledge further undermined any basis for distinguishing right from wrong. Darwinism appears to shatter the older understanding of man as a being distinguishable in kind, not merely by degree, from the other animals. Advances in physics suggest that everything in the universe, including man, is just a collection of particles, leaving humanity with no intrinsic specialness or dignity. Modern neuroscience claims that free will, or human choice, is an illusion.

Original Progressivism long ago left the field without having resolved any of these difficulties. Still, since human beings by nature want to proclaim some things good and others bad, a new claim to justice had to be asserted – and so was, by post-1960s leftism, about which it is hard to find anything good to say. At best, one can acknowledge that certain genuine injustices targeted by that movement did, indeed, demand correction. Yet all of these – above all the legacies of slavery and Jim Crow – were already being addressed through constitutional means. That is, until post-1960s leftism took over, with solutions incoherent in theory and destructive in practice.

First, "genuine equality" as posited by "justice as fairness" is not equality as understood from the American founding until the 1960 but is instead a leveling equality. Perhaps less obviously, "justice as fairness" does great violence to the concept of the common good. The common good as traditionally understood – policies that benefit the whole citizenry, enacted by lawful majorities – can under this new understanding no longer be a lodestar for politics because the majority – at least unless and until it is replaced by a new, more deserving majority – is by definition "privileged." The foremost purpose of politics shifts from securing the common good of all citizens to securing the particular good of groups held to be oppressed or disadvantaged. The idea of the common good is discarded, or else redefined so that the elimination of disadvantage *is* the common good. Virtue is redefined as that which helps the disadvantaged, including simply holding the correct opinions about disadvantage. Moderation, courage, and wisdom are nothing – perhaps are even vices – absent correct opinion and superfluous in its presence.

"Social justice" theory does even greater violence to true justice. As we have seen, there are only three possible bases for justice: reason, revelation, or will. Post-1960s leftism rejects revelation without so much as a thought. It is ambivalent about will. On the one hand, it grasps that its own rejection of traditional moral reasoning leaves no consistent ground for questioning will and knows that it owes many of its greatest triumphs to the assertion of will. On the other hand, it also intuits that recourse to will alone is somehow insufficient or unseemly. Hence it prefers to believe itself to be fully rational, and even "scientific."

This self-congratulation is unfounded. First, because the Left's relationship with science is tenuous at best. Leftists know that their grip on power is strengthened when their claims possess the veneer of scientific prestige and respectability. So they strive always to package their claims to justice in the language of science. This is why the highest sources of moral authority in our time are peer-reviewed articles written by research university faculty. Since the Left's hold on the universities is stronger than that of medieval monks on the monasteries, in practice this amounts to the Left approving the Left, vouching for one unreplicable study after another, in an endless echo chamber – or perhaps better to say "feedback loop," since the noise becomes ever louder and shriller.

But the Left also knows that science is not a reliable ally. Sometimes scientific conclusions support a moral claim or policy goal on behalf of the "disadvantaged," but often they don't. When they do, they are held to be unquestionable. Yet as one controversy after another has shown, any time a scientific conclusion – no matter how rigorous its basis – undermines or contradicts a leftist claim, it is not merely rejected but denounced. The Left increasingly goes so far as to insist that certain lines of scientific inquiry are simply immoral to pursue. Science must be subordinated to the moral claims and goals of "social justice," which are the true authority or highest value.

Second, post-1960s leftism stands or falls by the concept of "group rights," which is morally and logically incoherent. A right is a moral claim that all individuals justly hold vis-à-vis all other individuals, enforced – if at all – by their common government. If all men are created equal, they must be endowed by their Creator with equal natural rights. If some men by virtue of group membership – that is to say, by birth – have more or greater rights than others, then men are inherently unequal. "Group rights" in practice equals de facto aristocracy. It demands a sort of caste system – something leftists used to insist they were against – in which people are designated as better and worse according to lineage. (As an aside, we may note the irony that ardent social justice warriors make essentially the same claim as slavery's greatest defenders.)

In a republic, "group rights" inevitably lead to faction and the destruction of internal peace. Especially when viewed as resulting from hereditary guilt, the concept requires that the innocent living be held perpetually accountable for the sins of the (actually or allegedly) guilty dead. It means that some people are innately bad, simply according to birth, no matter what they actually *do* or *do not* do. This notion is antithetical to any conception of moral responsibility, of individual culpability or rectitude.

In truth, the post-1960s Left co-opts the language of "justice" and "rights" as a rhetorical device to get what it wants: the transfer of power, honor, and wealth between groups as retribution for past offenses. Since the concept of "social justice" denies both natural rights and revelation, its real basis is simply will: we want these things, therefore we say they are good. We don't like you, therefore we say you are bad.

The practical wreckage from this understanding of justice has been immense: a decades-long crime spree, launched by liberal leniency, that was only partially brought under control at great cost, and only after taking hundreds of thousands of lives (and that appears to be resurging, at least in certain cities, where homicides have recently risen for the first time since the late 1980s); the sexual revolution, which appears to be on track to destroy the family in every segment of society below the upper middle class, has deprived millions of children of a stable home, and made millions of both sexes lonely and miserable; the collapse of the universities, especially the humanities and social sciences, which trivialize and despise their ostensible subject matter while propagandizing students to hate their country; ongoing mass immigration that enriches the tippy-top of the socioeconomic ladder while imposing the costs on everyone else and "fundamentally transforms" one American community after another; foreign policy weakness and an inability to win wars, coupled with foolish overextension and hubris; limitless government expansion and intrusiveness; increasing restrictions on speech and thought, including the "unpersoning" of dissidents, and campaigns to turn heterodox thoughts and guilt by association (something else the Left used to insist it was strongly against) into grounds for unemployability for life.

Persecution and the Art of Shouting

This suppression of speech and thought is the second-most sinister feature of modern leftism. If we are to overcome it, we must understand its roots.

The first and most obvious is that, because "social justice" rests on a fallacy, it must suppress awareness of that fallacy. The leftist enterprise has staked its success on an absurd and obviously false account of inequality, viz., that all inequality is the result of injustice or oppression. There are only two ways to maintain public support for a proposition that is obviously false: compound the lies, or suppress and punish dissent. Indeed, the two go together because the more the lies pile up, the more dissent must be suppressed.

Since evidence for widespread present injustice is, to say the least, not altogether obvious, social justice warriors must insist that a great deal of present disadvantage is caused by past injustice. Since this assertion is undermined by many observable facts and by logic, it is not readily accepted by most of those held to be advantaged. Questions that inevitably arise include: Have we really disproved *all* possible explanations for disadvantage besides oppression? Are we absolutely certain that environmental, cultural, or personal factors play no role whatsoever? To the extent that such factors do not arise from one group of humans oppressing another, how can their effects be rightly called unjust? What reason do we have to believe that politics is even capable of eliminating inequalities that do not arise from oppression? What about the opportunity costs and waste that inevitably flow from attempts to accomplish the impossible? How much of today's disadvantage or inequality is truly attributable to injustices committed decades or even centuries ago? How can a person who has committed no injustice himself be responsible for the injustice of others? Even if one were to accept the concept of hereditary guilt, how can persons with no hereditary connection to past oppressors be responsible for their misdeeds?

These lines of inquiry more than suggest that redistribution and other efforts to correct all disadvantage are unjustified and counterproductive. Therefore, social justice warriors insist that said lines of inquiry be disallowed, along with any arguments that undermine public support for any element of their project. Such arguments are to be denounced when stated and their advocates punished to discourage further heresy. Here is the leftist saint Herbert Marcuse on the necessity of "repressive tolerance":

> *the withdrawal of toleration of speech and assembly from groups and movements which promote aggressive policies, armament, chauvinism, discrimination on the grounds of race and religion, or which oppose the extension of public services, social security, medical care, etc. Moreover, the restoration of freedom of thought may necessitate new and rigid restrictions on teachings and practices in the educational institutions which, by their very methods and*

concepts, serve to enclose the mind within the established universe of discourse and behavior – thereby precluding a priori a rational evaluation of the alternatives.

Once all claims to moral authority are vested in "history" and "science," secular persecution of heterodoxy follows almost inevitably. "History," recall, *is* progress – from worse to better. Who argues against the better? "Science" deals with true facts: verifiable, established, "settled" facts – the undeniable. Who denies the undeniable? To question history or dispute the conclusions of science is therefore to raise one's hand and proclaim "I'm insane!" One may pity the insane, but one has a duty not to allow insanity to spread, and also – to the extent possible – to correct the insane for their own good. They naturally may not always accept the correction as well-intended, but what do you expect? They're insane! This is, not coincidentally, the same way that medieval inquisitors treated heresy.

Furthermore, to question the moral claims of "history" – to ask whether the "debt that can never be repaid" is in fact actually owed, or whether the attempt at repayment might not be worth the immense costs – is to proclaim oneself not merely insane but evil. This helps explain the Left's increasing moralistic vindictiveness toward any questioning of its claims, and its fury at outright dissent.

Finally, the Left knows that it is in a difficult rhetorical position. The heart of its argument is that some people are inherently innocent and good while others are inherently guilty and bad and must be treated accordingly. To ears insufficiently attuned to the new understanding of justice, this can sound unjust. Tying moral worth to circumstances of birth?

Not treating people equally? Punishing the living for the sins of the dead? Why all this is – contrary to appearances, logic, and common sense – "just" requires considerable explanation. To the extent that people "get it," they will sharply divide between those who say that the "advantaged" have it coming and those who object "No, I don't."

The problem for the Left, therefore, is that while its message is very effective at egging on its own side, it can be equally effective at alarming and rousing its targets. The ideal solution would be to come up with a public message that rallies the Left while lulling its targets, but this turns out to be very difficult, if not impossible.

The next best thing is to forbid the targets from speaking up – with "speaking up" understood to include simply repeating the Left's rhetoric. Thus a commonplace *contretemps* of our time runs according to the following script: some leftist condemns an entire demographic group, often including a wish that harm befall it; she receives loud applause from the Left and from the ambient culture; a non-leftist repeats what she said and is denounced. The denunciation ensues whether or not the non-leftist adds any critical comments. His real offense is noticing, or more precisely noticing without celebrating. It's OK to notice if noticing takes the form of acknowledging justified anger and welcoming as deserved punishment whatever comes next. But noticing is very bad if it suggests even a hint of moral condemnation or – worse – the beginnings of organized opposition.

We may sum up the typical response of a leftist caught red-handed thus: "You're completely paranoid. That's not our plan at all; and even if it were, you'd have nothing to fear. Still, the fact that you're worried shows that you have a guilty conscience and deserve whatever it is we promise we're not going to do to you. Your talking about what we say is evidence of your badness. Stop talking about us, lest you force us to do to you what we insist it never even occurred to us to do."

The Left allows only three responses to its rhetoric: silence, agreement, or denial. As to this last, long experience has taught leftists that, whenever they blurt out what's really on their mind, they can count on "conservatives" to grope for ways to excuse or provisionally understand their hate speech – nothing to worry about! harmless hyperbole! – or, that failing, to assert moral equivalence with the president's tweets. (Meanwhile if an obscure yet genuine conservative merely says "If attacked, I will defend myself," he is denounced – by "conservatives" at least as vociferously as by leftists – as Literally Hitler.)

It is an odd feature of the current year that calling an avowed enemy a liar – publicly insisting that her plain words could not possibly mean what they plainly say – not only fails to provoke an angry denial but is welcomed by the alleged liar herself. Anything to keep leftism's targets somnambulant for as long as possible. The more Americans who wake up and realize that contemporary leftism is a revenge plot with themselves as its targets, the more will object and try to stop it. This is what the Left, at present, most fears and is trying to prevent.

The Choice We Face Now

But by far the most sinister feature of post-1960s leftism – the one that feeds all the others – is the spiritual sickness, the self-loathing and existential despair, with which it has infected the formerly confident and capable West. That sickness has been noticed and decried by figures ranging from Leo Strauss to Aleksandr Solzhenitsyn to Ronald Reagan. We define ourselves now solely by our past sins – real, exaggerated, and imagined. Those said to be "advantaged" or "privileged" are nothing more than the sum of their ancestors' transgressions and their own permanent inability to atone. It's understandable why the Left preaches this poison. Harder to understand is why so many millions accept it as gospel truth.

The fundamental choice we face in our time is whether to maintain the consensus in favor of self-loathing and self-destruction or return to life and the conditions of life: the rule of law, responsible freedom, confidence in our civilization, patriotism, and concern for the common good instead of only the particular good of groups claiming oppression or disadvantage. President Trump stated the matter with utmost clarity in Warsaw: "The fundamental question of our time is whether the West has the will to survive."

What I have summarized as "the American solution" is now treated by most elites – and all intellectual elites – as inherently evil. Democracy is no longer defined as government "of the people, by the people, for the people." Instead it is government of the people, by left-liberal experts and oligarchs, without consent. Globalism, wide-open trade, financialization, mass immigration, foreign war without end or clear connection to the national interest (to say nothing of victory), promotion of the left-liberal social agenda at home and abroad – all these are simply held to be nonnegotiable. Dissent is punished.

It should now be beyond obvious that what we have known as "conservatism" has failed at the task encapsulated in its very name. Its task going forward – for those remaining conservative intellectuals who have not formally or functionally defected to the Left – is to relearn, or learn for the first time, *what* to conserve, *why* it is worth conserving, and *how* to conserve it. The present study is a modest contribution toward helping with that task. I hope it will be received in that spirit.

THE FLIGHT 93 ELECTION

Publius Decius Mus

September 5, 2016

2016 is the Flight 93 election: charge the cockpit or you die. You may die anyway. You – or the leader of your party – may make it into the cockpit and not know how to fly or land the plane. There are no guarantees.

Except one: if you don't try, death is certain. To compound the metaphor: a Hillary Clinton presidency is Russian Roulette with a semi-auto. With Trump, at least you can spin the cylinder and take your chances.

To ordinary conservative ears, this sounds histrionic. The stakes can't be that high because they are never that high – except perhaps in the pages of Gibbon. Conservative intellectuals will insist that there has been no "end of history" and that all human outcomes are still possible. They will even – as Charles Kesler does – admit that America is in "crisis." But how great is the crisis? Can things really be so bad if eight years of Obama can be followed by eight more of Hillary, and yet constitutionalist conservatives can still reasonably hope for a restoration of our cherished ideals? Cruz in 2024!

Not to pick (too much) on Kesler, who is less unwarrantedly optimistic than most conservatives. And who, at least, poses the right question: Trump or Hillary? Though his answer – "even if [Trump] had chosen his policies at random, they would be sounder than Hillary's" – is unwarrantedly ungenerous. The truth is that Trump articulated, if incompletely and inconsistently, the right stances on the right issues – immigration, trade, and war – right from the beginning.

But let us back up. One of the paradoxes – there are so many – of conservative thought over the last decade at least is the unwillingness even to *entertain* the possibility that America and the West are on a trajectory toward something very bad. On the one hand, conservatives routinely present a litany of ills plaguing the body politic. Illegitimacy. Crime. Massive, expensive, intrusive, out-of-control government. Politically correct McCarthyism. Ever-higher taxes and ever-deteriorating services and infrastructure. Inability to win wars against tribal, sub–Third World foes. A disastrously awful educational system that churns out kids who don't know anything and, at the primary and secondary levels, can't (or won't) discipline disruptive punks, and at the higher levels saddles students with six-figure debts for the privilege. And so on and drearily on. Like that portion of the mass where the priest asks for your private intentions, fill in any dismal fact about American decline that you want and I'll stipulate it.

Conservatives spend at least several hundred million dollars a year on think tanks, magazines, conferences, fellowships, and such, complaining about this, that, the other, and everything. And yet these same conservatives are, at root, keepers of the status quo. Oh, sure, they want some things to change. They want their pet ideas adopted – tax deductions for having more babies and the like. Many of them are even good ideas. But are any of them truly fundamental? Do they get to the heart of our problems?

If conservatives are right about the importance of virtue, morality, religious faith, stability, character and so on in the individual; if they are right about sexual morality or what came to be termed "family values"; if they are right about the importance of education to inculcate good character and to teach the fundamentals that have defined knowledge in the West for millennia; if they are right about societal norms and public order; if they are right about the centrality of initiative, enterprise, industry, and thrift to a sound economy and a healthy society; if they are right about the soul-sapping effects of paternalistic Big Government and its cannibalization of civil society and religious institutions; if they are right about the necessity of a strong defense and prudent statesmanship in the international sphere – if they are right about the importance of all this to national health and even survival, then they must believe – mustn't they? – that *we are headed off a cliff*.

But it's quite obvious that conservatives don't believe any such thing, that they feel no such sense of urgency, of an immediate necessity to change course and avoid the cliff. A recent article by Matthew Continetti may be taken as representative – indeed, almost written for the purpose of illustrating the point.[1] Continetti inquires into the "condition of

---

1 Matthew Continetti, "The 'Condition of America' Question," *Weekly Standard*, August 5, 2016.

America" and finds it wanting. What does Continetti propose to do about it? The usual litany of "conservative" "solutions," with the obligatory references to decentralization, federalization, "civic renewal," and – of course! – Burke. Which is to say, conservatism's typical combination of the useless and inapt with the utopian and unrealizable. Decentralization and federalism are all well and good, and as a conservative, I endorse them both without reservation. But how are they going to save, or even meaningfully improve, the America that Continetti describes? What can they do against a tidal wave of dysfunction, immorality, and corruption? "Civic renewal" would do a lot of course, but that's like saying health will save a cancer patient. A step has been skipped in there somewhere. How are we going to *achieve* "civic renewal"? Wishing for a tautology to enact itself is not a strategy.

Continetti trips over a more promising approach when he writes of "stress[ing] the 'national interest abroad and national solidarity at home' through foreign-policy retrenchment, 'support to workers buffeted by globalization,' and setting 'tax rates and immigration levels' to foster social cohesion." That sounds a lot like Trumpism. But the phrases that Continetti quotes are taken from Ross Douthat and Reihan Salam, both of whom, like Continetti, are vociferously – one might even say fanatically – anti-Trump. At least they, unlike Kesler, give Trump credit for having identified the right stance on today's most salient issues. Yet, paradoxically, they won't vote for Trump whereas Kesler hints that he will. It's reasonable, then, to read into Kesler's esoteric endorsement of Trump an implicit acknowledgment that the crisis is, indeed, pretty dire. I expect a Claremont scholar to be wiser than most other conservative intellectuals, and I am relieved not to be disappointed in this instance.

Yet we may also reasonably ask: What explains the Pollyanna-ish declinism of so many others? That is, the stance that Things-Are-Really-Bad – But-Not-So-Bad-that-We-Have-to-Consider-Anything-Really-Different! The obvious answer is that they don't really believe the first half of that formulation. If so, like Chicken Little, they should stick a sock in it. Pecuniary reasons also suggest themselves, but let us foreswear recourse to this explanation until we have disproved all the others.

Whatever the reason for the contradiction, there can be no doubt that there *is* a contradiction. To simultaneously hold conservative cultural, economic, and political beliefs – to insist that our liberal-left present reality and future direction is incompatible with human nature and must undermine society – and yet also believe that things can go on more or less the way they are going, ideally but not necessarily with some conservative tinkering here and there, is logically impossible.

Let's be very blunt here: if you genuinely think things can go on with no fundamental change needed, then you have implicitly admitted that conservatism is wrong. Wrong philosophically, wrong on human nature, wrong on the nature of politics, and wrong in its policy prescriptions. Because, first, few of those prescriptions are in force today. Second, of the ones that are, the Left is busy undoing them, often with conservative assistance. And, third, the whole trend of the West is ever-leftward, ever further away from what we all understand as conservatism.

If your answer – Continetti's, Douthat's, Salam's, and so

many others' – is for conservatism to keep doing what it's been doing – another policy journal, another article about welfare reform, another half-day seminar on limited government, another tax credit proposal – even though we've been losing ground for at least a century, then you've implicitly accepted that your supposed political philosophy doesn't matter and that civilization will carry on just fine under leftist tenets. Indeed, that leftism is truer than conservatism and superior to it.

They will say, in words reminiscent of dorm-room Marxism – but our proposals have *not* been tried! Here our ideas sit, waiting to be implemented! To which I reply: eh, not really. Many conservative solutions – above all welfare reform and crime control – *have* been tried, and proved effective, but have nonetheless failed to stem the tide. Crime, for instance, is down from its mid-'70s and early '90s peak – but way, way up from the historic American norm that ended when liberals took over criminal justice in the mid-'60s. And it's rising fast today, in the teeth of ineffectual conservative complaints. And what has this temporary crime (or welfare, for that matter) decline done to stem the greater tide? The tsunami of leftism that still engulfs our every – literal and figurative – shore has receded not a bit but indeed has grown. All your (our) victories are short-lived.

More to the point, what has conservatism achieved *lately*? In the last twenty years? The answer – which appears to be "nothing" – might seem to lend credence to the plea that "our ideas haven't been tried." Except that the same conservatives who generate those ideas are in charge of selling them to the broader public. If their ideas "haven't been tried," who is ultimately at fault? The whole enterprise of Conservatism,

Inc., reeks of failure. Its sole recent and ongoing success is its own self-preservation. Conservative intellectuals never tire of praising "entrepreneurs" and "creative destruction." Dare to fail! they exhort businessmen. Let the market decide! Except, um, not with respect to us. Or is their true market not the political arena, but the fundraising circuit?

Only three questions matter. First, how bad are things really? Second, what do we do right now? Third, what should we do for the long term?

Conservatism, Inc.'s, "answer" to the first may, at this point, simply be dismissed. If the conservatives wish to have a serious debate, I for one am game – more than game; eager. The problem of "subjective certainty" can only be overcome by going into the agora. But my attempt to do so – the blog that Kesler mentions – was met largely with incredulity. How can they say that?! How can anyone apparently of our caste (conservative intellectuals) not merely *support* Trump (however lukewarmly) but offer *reasons* for doing so?

One of the *Journal of American Greatness*'s deeper arguments was that only in a corrupt republic, in corrupt times, could a Trump rise. It is therefore puzzling that those most horrified by Trump are the least willing to consider the possibility that the republic is dying. That possibility, apparently, seems to them so preposterous that no refutation is necessary.

As does, presumably, the argument that the stakes in 2016 are – everything. I should here note that I am a good deal gloomier than my (former) *JAG* colleagues, and that while we frequently used the royal "we" when discussing things on which we all agreed, I here speak only for myself.

How have the last two decades worked out for you, personally? If you're a member or fellow-traveler of the Davos class, chances are: pretty well. If you're among the subspecies conservative intellectual or politician, you've accepted – perhaps not consciously, but unmistakably – your status on the roster of the Washington Generals of American politics. Your job is to show up and lose, but you are a necessary part of the show and you do get paid. To the extent that you are ever on the winning side of anything, it's as sophists who help the Davoisie oligarchy rationalize open borders, lower wages, outsourcing, deindustrialization, trade giveaways, and endless, pointless, winless war.

All of Trump's sixteen Republican competitors would have ensured more of the same – as will the election of Hillary Clinton. That would be bad enough. But at least Republicans are merely reactive when it comes to wholesale cultural and political change. Their "opposition" may be in all cases ineffectual and often indistinguishable from support. But they don't dream up inanities like thirty-two "genders," elective bathrooms, single-payer, Iran sycophancy, "Islamophobia," and Black Lives Matter. They merely help ratify them.

A Hillary presidency will be pedal-to-the-metal on the entire progressive-Left agenda, plus items few of us have yet imagined in our darkest moments. Nor is even that the worst. It will be coupled with a level of vindictive persecution against resistance and dissent hitherto seen in the supposedly liberal West only in the most "advanced" Scandinavian countries and the most leftist corners of Germany and England. We see this already in the censorship practiced by the Davoisie's social media enablers; in the shameless propaganda tidal wave of the mainstream media; and in the personal destruction campaigns – operated through the former and aided by the latter – of the social justice warriors. We see it in Obama's flagrant use of the IRS to torment political opponents, the gaslighting denial by the media, and the collective shrug by everyone else.

It's absurd to assume that any of this would stop or slow – would do anything other than massively intensify – in a Hillary administration. It's even more ridiculous to expect that hitherto useless conservative opposition would suddenly become effective. For two generations at least, the Left has been calling everyone to their right Nazis. This trend has accelerated exponentially in the last few years, helped along by some on the right who really do seem to merit – and even relish – the label. There is nothing the modern conservative fears more than being called "racist," so alt-right pocket Nazis are manna from heaven for the Left. But also wholly unnecessary: sauce for the goose. The Left was calling us Nazis long before any pro-Trumpers tweeted Holocaust denial memes. And how does one deal with a Nazi – that is, with an enemy one is convinced intends your destruction? You don't compromise with him or leave him alone. You crush him.

So what do we have to lose by fighting back? Only our Washington Generals jerseys – and paychecks. But those are going away anyway. Among the many things the "Right" still doesn't understand is that the Left has concluded that this particular show need no longer go on. They don't think they need a foil anymore and would rather dispense with the whole bother of staging these phony contests in which each side ostensibly has a shot.

If you haven't noticed, our side has been losing consistently since 1988. We can win midterms, but we do nothing with them. Call ours Hannibalic victories. After the

Carthaginian's famous slaughter of a Roman army at Cannæ, he failed to march on an undefended Rome, prompting his cavalry commander to complain: "you know how to win a victory, but not how to use one." And, aside from 2004's lackluster 50.7 percent, we can't win the big ones at all.

Because the deck is stacked overwhelmingly against us. I will mention but three ways. First, the opinion-making elements – the universities and the media above all – are wholly corrupt and wholly opposed to everything we want, and increasingly even to our existence. (What else are the wars on "cis-genderism" – formerly known as "nature" – and on the supposed "white privilege" of broke hillbillies really about?) If it hadn't been abundantly clear for the last fifty years, the campaign of 2015–2016 must surely have made it evident to even the meanest capacities that the intelligentsia – including all the organs through which it broadcasts its propaganda – is overwhelmingly partisan and biased. Against this onslaught, "conservative" media is a nullity, barely a whisper. It cannot be heard above the blaring of what has been aptly called "The Megaphone."

Second, our Washington Generals self-handicap and self-censor to an absurd degree. Lenin is supposed to have said that "the best way to control the opposition is to lead it ourselves." But with an opposition like ours, why bother? Our "leaders" and "dissenters" bend over backward to play by the self-sabotaging rules the Left sets for them. Fearful, beaten dogs have more *thymos*.

Third and most important, the ceaseless importation of Third World foreigners with no tradition of, taste for, or experience in liberty means that the electorate grows more left, more Democratic, less Republican, less republican, and less traditionally American with every cycle. As does, of course, the U.S. population, which only serves to reinforce the two other causes outlined above. This is the core reason why the Left, the Democrats, and the bipartisan junta (categories distinct but very much overlapping) think they are on the cusp of a permanent victory that will forever obviate the need to pretend to respect democratic and constitutional niceties. Because they are.

It's also why they treat open borders as the "absolute value," the one "principle" that – when their "principles" collide – they prioritize above all the others. If *that* fact is insufficiently clear, consider this. Trump is the most liberal Republican nominee since Thomas Dewey. He departs from conservative orthodoxy in so many ways that *National Review* still hasn't stopped counting. But let's stick to just the core issues animating his campaign. On trade, globalization, and war, Trump is to the left (conventionally understood) not only of his own party, but of his Democratic opponent. And yet the Left and the junta are at one with the housebroken conservatives in their determination – desperation – not merely to defeat Trump but to destroy him. What gives?

Oh, right – there's that *other* issue. The sacredness of mass immigration is the mystic chord that unites America's ruling and intellectual classes. Their reasons vary somewhat. The Left and the Democrats seek ringers to form a permanent electoral majority. They, or many of them, also believe the academic-intellectual lie that America's inherently racist and evil nature can be expiated only through ever greater "diversity." The junta of course craves cheaper and more docile labor. It also seeks to legitimize, and deflect unwanted attention from, its wealth and power by pretending that its open borders stance is a form of *noblesse oblige*. The Republicans and the "conservatives"? Both of course desperately want absolution from the charge of "racism." For the latter, this at least makes some sense. No Washington General can take the court – much less cash his check – with that epithet dancing over his head like some Satanic Spirit. But for the former, this priestly grace comes at the direct expense of their worldly interests. Do they honestly believe that the right enterprise zone or charter school policy will arouse 50.01 percent of our newer voters to finally reveal their "natural conservatism" at the ballot box? It hasn't happened anywhere yet and shows no signs that it ever will. But that doesn't stop the Republican refrain: more, more, more! No matter how many elections they lose, how many districts tip forever blue, how rarely (if ever) their immigrant vote cracks 40 percent, the answer is always the same. Just like Angela Merkel after yet another rape, shooting, bombing, or machete attack. More, more, more!

This is insane. This is the mark of a party, a society, a country, a people, a civilization that wants to die. Trump, alone among candidates for high office in this or in the last seven (at least) cycles, has stood up to say: I want to live. I want my party to live. I want my country to live. I want my people to live. I want to end the insanity.

Yes, Trump is worse than imperfect. So what? We can lament until we choke the lack of a great statesman to address the fundamental issues of our time – or, more importantly, to connect them. Since Pat Buchanan's three failures, occasionally a candidate arose who saw one piece: Dick Gephardt on trade, Ron Paul on war, Tom Tancredo on immigration. Yet, among recent political figures – great statesmen, dangerous demagogues, and mewling gnats alike – only Trump-the-alleged-buffoon not merely saw all three and their essential connectivity, *but was able to win on them*. The alleged buffoon is thus more prudent – more practically wise – than all of our wise-and-good who so bitterly oppose him. This should embarrass them. That their failures instead embolden them is only further proof of their foolishness and hubris.

Which they self-laud as "consistency" – adherence to "conservative principle," defined by the 1980 campaign and the household gods of reigning conservative think tanks. A higher consistency in the service of the national interest apparently eludes them. When America possessed a vast, empty continent and explosively growing industry, high immigration was arguably good policy. (*Arguably*: Ben Franklin would disagree.)[2] It hasn't made sense since World War I. Free trade was unquestionably a great boon to the American worker in the decades after World War II. We long ago passed the point of diminishing returns. The Gulf War of 1991 was a strategic victory for American interests. No conflict since then has been. Conservatives either can't see this – or, worse, those who can nonetheless treat the only political leader to mount a serious challenge to the status quo (more immigration, more trade, more war) as a unique evil.

Trump's vulgarity is in fact a godsend to the conservatives. It allows them to hang their public opposition on his obvious shortcomings and to ignore or downplay his far greater strengths, which should be even more obvious but in

---

2 Benjamin Franklin, "Observations Concerning the Increase of Mankind," 1751.

corrupt times can be deliberately obscured by constant references to his faults. That the Left would make the campaign all about the latter is to be expected. Why would the Right? Some – a few – are no doubt sincere in their belief that the man is simply unfit for high office. David Frum, who has always been an immigration skeptic and is a convert to the less-war position, is sincere when he says that, even though he agrees with much of Trump's agenda, he cannot stomach Trump. But for most of the other #NeverTrumpers, is it just a coincidence that they also happen to favor Invade the World, Invite the World?

Another question *JAG* raised without provoking any serious attempt at refutation was whether, in corrupt times, it took a … let's say … "loudmouth" to rise above the din of The Megaphone. We, or I, speculated: "yes." Suppose there had arisen some statesman of high character – dignified, articulate, experienced, knowledgeable – the exact opposite of everything the conservatives claim to hate about Trump. Could this hypothetical paragon have won on Trump's same issues? Would the conservatives have supported him? I would have – even had he been a Democrat.

Back on planet earth, that flight of fancy at least addresses what to do now. The answer to the subsidiary question – will it work? – is much less clear. By "it" I mean Trumpism, broadly defined as secure borders, economic nationalism, and America-first foreign policy. We Americans have chosen, in our foolishness, to disunite the country through stupid immigration, economic, and foreign policies. The level of unity America enjoyed before the bipartisan junta took over can never be restored.

But we can probably do better than we are doing now.

First, stop digging. No more importing poverty, crime, and alien cultures. We have made institutions, by leftist design, not merely abysmal at assimilation but abhorrent of the concept. We should try to fix that, but given the Left's iron grip on every school and cultural center, that's like trying to bring democracy to Russia. A worthy goal, perhaps, but temper your hopes – and don't invest time and resources unrealistically.

By contrast, simply building a wall and enforcing immigration law will help enormously, by cutting off the flood of newcomers that perpetuates ethnic separatism and by incentivizing the English language and American norms in the workplace. These policies will have the added benefit of aligning the economic interests of, and (we may hope) fostering solidarity among, the working, lower middle, and middle classes of all races and ethnicities. The same can be said for Trumpian trade policies and antiglobalization instincts. Who cares if productivity numbers tick down, or if our already somnambulant GDP sinks a bit further into its pillow? Nearly all the gains of the last twenty years have accrued to the junta anyway. It would, at this point, be better for the nation to divide up more equitably a slightly smaller pie than to add one extra slice – only to ensure that it and eight of the other nine go first to the government and its rentiers, and the rest to the same four industries and two hundred families.

Will this work? Ask a pessimist, get a pessimistic answer. So don't ask. Ask instead: is it worth trying? Is it better than the alternative? If you can't say, forthrightly, "yes," you are either part of the junta, a fool, or a conservative intellectual.

And if it doesn't work, what then? We've established that most "conservative" anti-Trumpites are in the Orwellian sense objectively pro-Hillary. What about the rest of you? If you recognize the threat she poses, but somehow can't stomach him, have you thought about the longer term? The possibilities would seem to be: Cæsarism, secession / crack-up, collapse, or managerial Davoisie liberalism as far as the eye can see ... which, since nothing human lasts forever, at some point will give way to one of the other three. Oh, and, I suppose, for those who like to pour a tall one and dream big, a second American Revolution that restores constitutionalism, limited government, and a 28 percent top marginal rate.

But for those of you who are sober: can you sketch a more plausible long-term future than the prior four following a Trump defeat? I can't either.

The election of 2016 is a test – in my view, the final test – of whether there is any *virtù* left in what used to be the core of the American nation. If they cannot rouse themselves simply to vote for the first candidate in a generation who pledges to advance their interests, and to vote against the one who openly boasts that she will do the opposite (a million more Syrians, anyone?), then they are doomed. They may not deserve the fate that will befall them, but they will suffer it regardless.

RESTATEMENT ON FLIGHT 93

Publius Decius Mus

September 13, 2016

Well, that was unexpected.

Everything I said in "The Flight 93 Election" was derivative of things I had already said, with (I thought) more vim and vigor, in a now-defunct blog. I assumed the new piece would interest a handful of that blog's remaining fans and no one else. My predictive powers proved imperfect.

Which should cheer everyone who hated what I said: if I was wrong about the one thing, maybe I'm wrong about the others. But let me take the various objections in ascending order of importance.

First is the objection to anonymity and specifically to the pseudonym. Anonymity supposedly proves that I am a coward, while the use of "Decius" shows that I am a hypocrite. What am *I* risking? I freely admit that, unlike the real Decius, I don't expect to die. But I do have something to lose, and may well yet lose it. I could easily have not written anything.

How could speaking up possibly have been more cowardly than silence?

Second is the objection to my invoking Flight 93. I refer such objectors to Stanton's words at the death of Lincoln: "Now he belongs to the ages." Heroes always belong to the ages. For all of recorded history, men have drawn inspiration from, and made analogies to, their heroes. Speaking only of us Americans, for more than two hundred years, we've been making Bunker Hill analogies, Gettysburg and Pickett's Charge analogies, San Juan Hill, Belleau Wood, D-Day, Okinawa, Chosin Reservoir, Khe Sanh, and so on and on. But all of a sudden this is "disgusting." It's quite obvious that what's really disgusting to these objectors is Trump. Which they could say forthrightly without recourse to the cheap, left-wing tactic of feigned, selective outrage over a time-honored rhetorical device that goes back to the Greeks, which conservatives are perfectly happy to use when it suits their immediate interest.

Some also complained about the aptness of the analogy: the plane crashed! Well, yes, and this one might too. Then again, it might not. It depends in part on what action the electorate chooses to take. The passengers of Flight 93 roused themselves. They succeeded insofar as that plane did not hit its intended target. The temptation not to rouse oneself in a time of great peril is always strong. In another respect, the analogy is even more apt. All of the passengers on Flight 93 – and all of the victims at the World Trade Center and the Pentagon – died owing in part to a disastrously broken immigration system that didn't then and still doesn't serve the interests of the American people. Which also happens to be the core issue at stake in this election.

A third objection is that Trump is immoderate in the Aristotelian, or personal, sense and I don't take that into sufficient account. I have even been lambasted for acknowledging, but not going into detail on, Trump's faults – as if that theme hasn't been done to death elsewhere. Trump is not the statesman I would have chosen for this moment. My preferences run toward Washington, Lincoln, Churchill, Reagan, and the like. Trump doesn't measure up to any of them. But his flaws are overstated. One of the dumber things often said about Trump is that "you can't trust him with the nuclear codes." This statement, first, betrays a complete lack of understanding of nuclear command and control. More important, it's an extraordinary calumny, one that accuses the man of a wish or propensity to commit mass murder on the scale of Pol Pot. On what basis does anyone make such an accusation? Can Trump be erratic, obnoxious, and offensive? Of course, he can be all that and more. But while these qualities are not virtues, they may well have helped him punch through the Overton Window, in which case I am willing to make allowances.

For this objection to be decisive, Trump's personal immoderation would have to be on a level that aspires to tyrannical rule. I don't see it. Not even close. The charge of "buffoon" seems a million times more apt than "tyrant." And even so, one must wonder how buffoonish the alleged buffoon really is when he is right on the most important issues while so many others who are esteemed wise are wrong. Hillary Clinton launched the Libya war, perhaps the worst security policy mistake in U.S. history – which divided a country between two American enemies and anarchy, and took a stream of refugees into Europe and surged it into a flood.

She pledges to vastly increase the refugee flow from the Middle East into our communities (and, mark my words, they will be Red State communities). Trump by contrast promises not to launch misguided wars, to protect our borders, and to focus immigration policy on the well-being of the currently constituted American people. Who is truly more moderate: the colorful loudmouth with the sensible agenda or the corrupt, icy careerist with the radical agenda?

The fourth objection is that I, or what I advocate, am/is immoderate, dangerous, radical, imprudent, and so on. This is a large claim that will require significant exploration. To those of you who complained about the length of the other one, best to tune out now.

My use (once each) of the terms *thymos* and *virtù* was taken as evidence that I am advocating a politics of "great daring" or some such. I'd like to be generous here and just presume this is a misunderstanding. I suggest to anyone who holds this interpretation to look at the specific contexts in which those words were used. The former referred to go-along, get-along conservative intellectuals, who could do with a double dose of *thymos*. Several writers on the left obligingly made the point. Good conservatism adheres to the parameters we set for you. You may say this, but not this. If you do and say what we tell you to, your reward will be that we will call you racist Nazis a little less. Also, what we allow as "good conservatism" will drift ever leftward, so that something we permitted a year or two ago is subject to revocation without notice and you better get on board immediately or the deal is off. Conservatism has accepted this "bargain" – hence its lack of *thymos* – yet amazingly thinks of itself as standing firm for eternal principle. But when I write in praise of virtue, morality, religious faith, stability, character, education, social norms and public order, initiative, enterprise, industry and thrift, and prudent statesmanship; when I warn against paternalistic Big Government, the decay of our educational system, and the cannibalization of civil society and religious institutions – time-honored conservative themes all – the Left responds with "insane," "deranged," "chilling," and "poison." And the same conservatives who cite adherence to conservative principle as their reason for opposing Trump side with . . . the Left.

As for the reference to *virtù,* the context was my recommendation of that supremely radical and immoderate act of . . . voting. Has it come to this? Merely advocating that people *vote* for a candidate who promises to further their interests – and the nominee of one of the two major parties in a party system that traces back to 1800 at least – this is now immoderate and "daring."

That is of course exactly the way the Left wants to frame this election. The same way that they define for us what acceptable conservatism can and cannot be, they now assert the right to choose – or at least veto – our candidates. And we supinely go along.

A point from the earlier essay is worth repeating. Conservatives have shouted since the beginning of Trump's improbable rise: He's not one of us! He is *not* conservative! And, indeed, in many ways, Trump is downright liberal. You might think that would make him more acceptable to the Left. But no. As "compassionate conservatism" did nothing to blunt leftist hatred of George W. Bush, neither do Trump's quasi-liberal economic positions. In fact, they hate Trump much more. Trump is not conservative enough for the conservatives but way too conservative for the Left, yet somehow they find common cause. Earlier I posited that the reason is Trump's position on immigration. Let me add two others.

The first is simply that Trump might win. He is not playing his assigned role of gentlemanly loser the way McCain and Romney did, and may well have tapped into some previously untapped sentiment that he can ride to victory. This is a problem for both the Right and the Left. The professional Right (correctly) fears that a Trump victory will finally make their irrelevance undeniable. The Left knows that so long as Republicans kept playing by the same rules and appealing to the same dwindling base of voters, there was no danger. Even if one of the old breed had won, nothing much would have changed, since their positions on the most decisive issues were effectively the same as the Democrats and because they posed no serious challenge to the administrative state.

Which points to the far more important reason. I urge readers to go back through John Marini's argument,[1] to which I cannot do anything close to full justice. Suffice to say here, the current governing arrangement of the United States is rule by a transnational managerial class in conjunction with the administrative state. To the extent that the parties are adversarial at the national level, it is merely to determine who gets to run the administrative state for four years. Challenging the administrative state is out of the question. The Democrats are united on this point. The Republicans are at least nominally divided. But those nominally

---

[1] John Marini, "Donald Trump and the American Crisis," *Claremont Review of Books*, July 22, 2016.

opposed (to the extent that they even understand the problem, which is: not much) are unwilling or unable to actually do anything about it. Are challenges to the administrative state allowed only if they are guaranteed to be ineffectual? If so, the current conservative movement is tailor-made for the task. Meanwhile, the much stronger Ryan wing of the party actively abets the administrative state and works to further the managerial class agenda.

Trump is the first candidate since Reagan to threaten this arrangement. To again oversimplify Marini (and Aristotle), the question here is: who rules? The many or the few? The people or the oligarchs? Our Constitution says: the people are sovereign, and their rule is mediated through representative institutions, limited by written constitutional norms. The administrative state says: experts must rule because various advances (the march of history) have made governing too complicated for public deliberation, and besides, the unwise people often lack knowledge of their own best interests even on rudimentary matters. When the people want something that they shouldn't want or mustn't have, the administrative state prevents it, no matter what the people vote for. When the people don't want something that the administrative state sees as salutary or necessary, it is simply imposed by fiat.

Don't want more immigration? Too bad, we know what's best. Think bathrooms should be reserved for the two biological sexes? Too bad, we rule. And so on and on.

To all the "conservatives" yammering about my supposed opposition to constitutional principle (more on that below) and who hate Trump, I say: Trump is mounting the first serious national-political defense of the Constitution in a generation. He may not see himself in those terms. I believe he sees himself as a straightforward patriot who just wants to do what is best for his country and its people. Whatever the case, he is asserting the right of the sovereign people to make their government do what they want it to do, and not do things they don't want it to do, in the teeth of determined opposition from a managerial class and administrative state that want not merely different policies but above all to perpetuate their own rule.

If the Constitution has any force or meaning, then "We the People" get to decide not merely who gets to run the administrative state – which, whatever the outcome, will always continue on the same path – more fundamentally, we get to decide what policies we want and which we don't. Apparently, to the whole Left and much of the Right, this stance is immoderate and dangerous. The people who make that charge claim to do so in defense of constitutional principle. I can't square that circle. Can you?

(To those tempted to accuse me of advocating a crude majoritarianism, I refer you to what I said above and will say below on the proper, constitutional operation of the United States government as originally designed and improved by the pre-Progressive amendments.)

One must also wonder what is so "immoderate" about Trump's program. As noted, it's to the left of the last several decades of Republican-conservative orthodoxy. "Moderate" in the modern political (as opposed to the Aristotelean) sense tends to be synonymous with "centrist." By that definition, Trump is a moderate. That's why *National Review* and the rest of the conservatives came out of the gate so strongly against him. I admit that, not all that long ago, I probably would have too. But I have come to see conservatism in a different light. To oversimplify (again), the only "eternal principle" is the good. What, specifically, is good in a political context varies with the times and with circumstance, as does how best to achieve the good in a given context. The good is not tax rates or free trade. Those aren't even principles. In the American political context, the good is the well-being of the physical America and its people, well-being defined (in terms that reflect both Aristotle and the American founding) as their "safety and happiness." That's what conservatism should be working to conserve.

Trump seems to grasp that the best way to do so in these times is to promote more solidarity and unity. The "conservatives" by contrast think it means more individualism. Neither of these, either, is an eternal principle. Prudence calls for a balance. Few would want the maximized (and forced) unity of ancient Sparta or modern North Korea. Only fool libertarians seek the maximized individualism of Ayn Rand. No unity means no nation. No individualism means no liberty. In an actual republic, a balance must be maintained, which can require occasional course corrections. In 1980, after a decade of stagnation, we needed an infusion of individualism. In 2016, we are too fragmented and atomized – united for the most part only by being equally under the thumb of the administrative state – and desperately need more unity.

Which means that Trump, right now, is right and the conservatives are wrong. His moderate program of secure borders, economic nationalism, and America-first foreign policy – all things that liberals and conservatives alike used to take for granted, if they disagreed on implementation –

holds the promise of fostering more unity. But today, liberals are apoplectic at the mere mention of this program – controlling borders is "extreme" but a "borderless world" is the "ultimate wisdom" – and the Finlandized conservatives aid them in attacking the candidate who promotes it. Conservatives claim to deplore the way the Democrats slice and dice the electorate, reduce it to voting blocs and interest groups, and stoke resentments to boost turnout. But faced with a candidate explicitly running on a unity agenda they insist he is too extreme to trust with the reins of power. One wants to ask, again: which is it, conservatives? Is Trump to be rejected because he is too moderate or because he is too extreme? The answer appears to be that it doesn't matter, so long as Trump is rejected.

So that's my "immoderate" case for Trump: do things that are in the interests of lower, working, and middle class Americans in order to improve their lives and increase unity across all swaths and sectors of society. And in so doing, reassert the people's rightful, constitutional control of their government. "Dangerous." "Extreme." "Radical." "Poison." "Authoritarian."

Which points to the fifth objection: in giving reasons for Trump, I oppose the Constitution and support "authoritarianism." First of all, I don't even know what the latter is – beyond the discredited Adorno study that the Left still uses to tar everyone to its right as Nazis. If we simply go by the Wiki definition – "authoritarianism is a form of government characterized by strong central power and limited political freedoms" – that sounds to me much more like the administrative state than anything Trump has proposed. Or do you mean "fascist"? Then say so. I have some idea of what that is. Or do you mean "tyrant"? I certainly know what that is. Are you saying Trump is one, or wants to be, or that I welcome either?

More risible – downright intelligence-insulting – is to read liberals accuse conservatives of wanting to trash the Constitution. Really. The Left has been insisting for more than a century that our Constitution is fatally flawed, written for another age, outmoded, hypocritical, hopelessly undermined by slavery and racism and sexism and property requirements, and so much else. Conservatives who argue for originalism and strict construction and federalism – sticking exactly to the letter of the Constitution – are called racists because everyone supposedly knows that the former are mere "code words."

This is a very large topic, and for those interested, there is an equally large body of scholarship that explains it all in detail. For now, let's just ask ourselves two questions. First, how do the mechanics of government, as written in the Constitution, differ from current practice? Second, how well are the rights amendments observed? As to the first, we do still have those three branches of government mentioned. But we also have a fourth, hidden in plain sight within the executive, namely the bureaucracy or administrative state. It both usurps legislative power and uses executive power in an unaccountable way. Congress does not use its own powers but meekly defers to the executive and to the bureaucracy. The executive does whatever it wants. The judiciary also usurps legislative and, when it's really feeling its oats, executive power through the use of consent decrees and the like. And that's just the feds – before we even get to the relationship between the feds and the states. As to the second, can you think of a single amendment among the Bill of Rights that is not routinely violated – with the acquiescence and approval of the Left? I can't.

All this happened because, for more than a century, the Left has been working at best to "change" and "update" the Constitution, and at worst to ignore it or get around it. This agenda is not hidden but announced and boasted of. Yet when someone on the right points out that the Constitution – by design – no longer works as designed, that the U.S. government does not in practice function as a constitutional republic, we are lambasted as "authoritarian."

That's a malicious lie. The truth is that the Left pushed and dragged us here. *You* wanted this. We didn't. You didn't like the original Constitution. We did and do. You didn't want it to operate as designed because when it does it too often prevents you from doing what you want to do. So you actively worked to give the courts and the bureaucracy the last word, some of you for high-minded reasons of sincere conviction, but most of you simply because you know they're on your side. You said it would be better this way. When we opposed you, you called us "racists." Now that you've got what you wanted, and we acknowledge your success, you call us "authoritarian" and "anticonstitutionalist." This is gaslighting on the level of "If you like your health care, you can keep your health care." Exasperating and infuriating, yet impressive in its shamelessness. But that's the Left for you: *l'audace, l'audace – toujours l'audace.*

My argument was and is a lament. I differ in no respect from my conservative brethren in my reverence for constitutional government in general or for the United States Constitution in particular. No respect, it seems, but one. They seem to think we are one election away from turning everything around – only, you know, not 2016, but the next one when we can run Cruz. Whereas I fear we are one election away from losing the last vestiges forever.

Which brings me to the final two objections, which are really the same: I am said to be insane, and my insanity is supposedly evident from my contention that things are really bad, when in fact they are not that bad.

I would be overjoyed to read a convincing account of why things are not that bad, why – despite appearances – the republic is healthy, constitutional norms are respected, the working class and hinterland communities are in good shape, social pathologies are low or at least declining, our elites prioritize the common good, our intellectuals and the media are honest and fair. Or if that's too big a lift, how about one that acknowledges all the problems and outlines some reasonable prospect for renewal? But only if it's *believable*. No skipped steps and no magical thinking. Dr. Conservatism needs to do better than his habitual "Sorry about the cancer, here's a bottle of aspirin."

If someone writes such a piece, I promise to read it and try to be persuaded by it. You might be doing me – and others whom I have misguidedly misled – a great favor. Only a fool would choose pessimism for its own sake. In my case, it chose me, against my will, because in current circumstances it just seems more plausible – in greater alignment with the observable facts – than optimism. But if I'm wrong, have at it. That's what I meant by my reference to the agora. Arriving at the truth is hard enough with open, honest debate. It's impossible without it. So flay me, by all means, and I will try to learn something.

I would also be overjoyed to be persuaded that the country into which I was born, which I have always loved instinctively, and which I was taught to love at the deepest theoretical level, is not in grave peril. Or if it is, that it can be saved even after eight more years of "fundamental transformation" – which means administrative state consolidation and managerial class entrenchment.

Alas, my venture into the agora has not yet changed my mind. Every four years the electorate becomes more unfavorable to Republican candidates, owing above all to mass immigration, which so many Republicans still self-sabotagingly support. We could not even deny reelection to Barack Obama, whose first term was a dismal failure by every measure, because he was able to overwhelm us with sheer demographics. "Quantity has a quality all its own." It will be worse in 2020 than it is now in 2016, just as 2016 is worse than 2012. Not to get all Rubio on you, but they know exactly what they're doing.[2]

If Hillary wins, there will still be a country, in the sense of a geographic territory with a people, a government, and various institutions. Things will mostly look the same, just as – outwardly – Rome changed little on the ascension of Augustus. It will not be tyranny or Cæsarism – not yet. But it will represent, in my view, an irreversible triumph for the administrative state. Consider that no president has been denied reelection since 1992. If we can't beat the Democrats now, what makes anyone think we could in 2020, when they will have all the advantages of incumbency plus four more years of demographic change in their favor? And if we can't

2 In one of the presidential debates, Marco Rubio drew ridicule for repeatedly assuring us that Barack Obama "knows exactly what he's doing."

win in 2016 or 2020, what reason is there to hope for 2024? Will the electorate be more Republican? More conservative? Will constitutional norms be stronger?

The country will go on, but it will not be a constitutional republic. It will be a blue state on a national scale. Only one party will really matter. A Republican may win now and again – once in a generation, perhaps – but only a neutered one who has "updated" all his positions so as to be more in tune with the new electorate. I.e., who has done exactly what the Left has for years been concern-trolling us to do: move left and become more like them. Yet another irony: the "conservatives" who object to Trump as too liberal are working to guarantee that only a Republican far more liberal than Trump could ever win the presidency again.

Still and all, for many – potentially me included – life under perma-liberalism will be nice. If you are in the managerial class, you will probably do well – so long as you don't say the wrong thing. (And, as noted, the list of "wrong things" will be continuously updated, so make sure you keep up.)

Professional conservatives seem to believe that their prospects will remain yoked to that of the managerial class. Maybe, but I doubt it. Eventually their donors are going to wake up and figure out what the Democrats and the Left realized long ago: conservatives serve no purpose anymore. Then the money will dry up and – what then? To the extent that our "conservatives" soldier on *eo nomine*, life will be a lot worse for them than their current, comfortable status as Washington Generals. They will have to adjust to dhimmitude. I can't tell if they don't understand this, or do and accept it. Then again, what difference, at this point, would that make?

For the rest of you – flyover people – the decline will continue. But things are pretty bad now, yet you can still eat and most of you have cars, flat screens, and air conditioners. So what are you complaining about?

Keep in mind, this is the *best-case scenario*. Which leaves open the larger questions raised in the prior essay that gave so many the vapors: how long could that possibly last? And what follows when it ends? The #NeverTrumpers don't even attempt to answer the second because their implicit answer to the first is: forever. Who knew they were all closet Hegelians? Yet I'm called nuts for raising doubts.

Can we at least finally admit, squarely, that conservatism has failed? On the very terms that it set for itself? I don't mean that in an accusatory or celebratory way – I'm quite sad about it, honest! – only as a matter of plain fact.

One of those who most objected to the Flight 93 analogy also accused me of "sophistry." I remind him that, according to Aristotle, "the Sophists identified or almost identified politics with rhetoric. In other words, the Sophists believed or tended to believe in the omnipotence of speech." Is that not a near-perfect description of modern conservative intellectuals, or at least of their revealed preferences? Except that one wonders what, in their case, is the source of that belief, since they haven't been able to accomplish anything in the political realm through speech or any other means in a generation.

One can point to a few enduring successes: Tax rates haven't approached their former stratospheric highs. On the other hand, the Left is busy undoing welfare and policing reform. Beyond that, we've not been able to implement our agenda even when we win elections – which we do less and less. Conservatism had a project for national renewal that it failed to implement, while the Left made – and still makes – gain after gain after gain. Consider conservatism's aims: "civic renewal," "federalism," "originalism," "morality and family values," "small government," "limited government," "Judeo-Christian values," "strong national defense," "respect among nations," "economic freedom," "an expanding pie," "the American dream." I support all of that. And all of it has been in retreat for thirty years. At least. But conservatism cannot admit as much, not even to itself, in the middle of the night with the door closed, the lights out and no one listening.

I tried to tell it, and it got mad.

Acknowledgments

I am grateful to Roger Kimball and to Encounter Books for giving me the opportunity to state, in succinct yet sufficient form, my vision of the foundations of American greatness and the threats facing them. I also thank Roger for permission to republish, in somewhat different form, a portion of my article "Founding Philosophy" from the June 2018 issue of *The New Criterion*. I thank Carol Staswick for her conscientious, thorough and tireless editing, which prompted much rethinking and rewriting. If you find something in the new parts of this volume that doesn't make sense, don't blame her; she tried to warn me. I thank the *Claremont Review of Books* for permission to republish "The Flight 93 Election" and the "Restatement on Flight 93." I also thank my teachers, fellow students, and friends – many now teaching at Hillsdale College, most affiliated with the Claremont Institute – for their generosity and support over more than thirty years of ongoing inquiry. Naturally, I do not claim to speak for them, nor do I invoke them as authorities to vouch for my accuracy. Nonetheless, the more of them who agree (to one extent or another) with what I have written here, the more I will consider this exercise to have been successful.

A NOTE ON THE TYPE

AFTER THE FLIGHT 93 ELECTION has been set in Scala, a family of types originally designed in the 1990s by Martin Majoor. A distinctly contemporary face, Scala roman marries the proportions of old-style types to the monoline strokes of geometric sans-serifs and the slab serifs of so-called Egyptian faces. The especially pleasing harmony between roman and italic reveals the designer's attention to every detail of his design. Although its ancestry can be traced to no single family of types, Scala succeeds in a wide range of uses by virtue of its clean drawing, its vertical emphasis, and its personable, somewhat casual letterforms. ◇ The display type is Berthold's Akzidenz Grotesk Light Condensed, a twentieth-century addition to a highly regarded family of types whose origins date to 1896.

DESIGN & COMPOSITION BY CARL W. SCARBROUGH